W9-BHR-464

e
Macmillan Company

Howell Book House
No part of this book may be reproduced or transmitted in any
s, electronic or mechanical, including photocopying, recording,
n storage and retrieval system, without permission in writing from

istered trademark of Macmillan, Inc.

Cataloging-in-Publication Data

d Dog: An Owner's Guide to a Happy, Healthy Pet

al references.

ogs. I. Title.

)5-23974

ited States of America

ue De Vito
Felice Primeau
seau
himon

by Judith Strom
n Kennel Club: 18
n: 93

, 145
Paulette: 8, 30, 46, 61, 82
n Cocker Spaniels: 148

103, 111, 116–117, 122, 123, 127

27, 38–39, 45, 51, 75, 133

, 31, 33, 34, 40, 42, 43, 49, 54, 59, 60, 64, 77, 92, 96, 107,
9, 140, 144, 149, 150
rchill: 13, 65, 96–97
es, John Carroll, Jama Carter,
Coler, Victor Peterson, Terri Sheehan,
Angelis and Kathy Iwasaki

C
She

An

Howell Book Hous
A Simon & Schuste
1633 Broadway
New York, NY 1001

Copyright © 1995 b
All rights reserved.
form or by any mean
or by any informatio
the Publisher.

MACMILLAN is a re

Library of Congress (
Palika, Liz, 1954–
The German Shepher
p. cm.
Includes bibliographi

ISBN: 0-87605-382-7

1. German shepherd d
SF429.G37P35 1995
636.7'37—dc20
CIP

Manufactured in the U
10 9 8 7 6 5

Series Director: Dominic
Series Assistant Director
Book Design: Michele L
Cover Design: Iris Jerom
Illustration: Jeff Yesh
Photography:
 *Cover: Joan Balzarini, pu
 Courtesy of the Americ
 Courtesy of Ken-L Ratio
 Joan Balzarini: 66, 96
 Mary Bloom: 63, 96, 13
 Paulette Braun/Pets by
 Buckinghamhill America
 Sian Cox: 134
 Dr. Ian Dunbar: 98, 101,
 Dan Lyons: 96
 Cathy Merrithew: 129
 Liz Palika: 2–3, 7, 20, 25,
 Janice Raines: 132
 Judith Strom: 5, 11, 22, 29
 110, 128, 130, 135, 137, 1
 Kerrin Winter & Dale Chu
Production Team: Troy Barn
 Kathleen Caulfield, Trudy
 Marvin Van Tiem, Amy De

Contents

Welcome

to the

World

of the

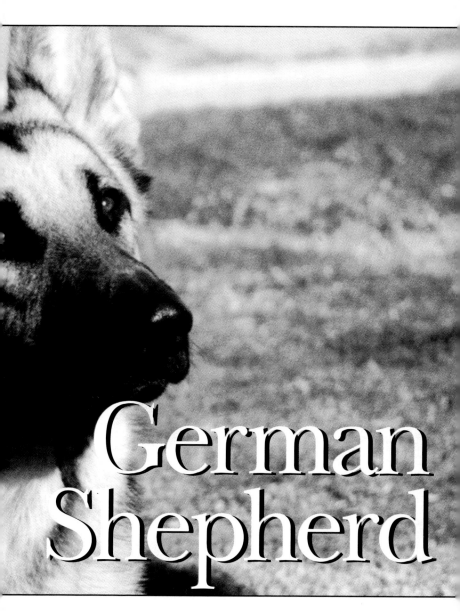

part one

German Shepherd

External Features of the German Shepherd Dog

Muzzle

Stop

Cheek

Skull

Shoulder

Crest

Neck

Wrist

Withers

Forearm

Elbow

Back

Pastern

Dewclaw

Stifle or Knee

Loin

Croup

Toes

Hock

chapter 1

What is a German Shepherd Dog?

Introduction to the Standard

What is a standard? Each breed of dog that is recognized by the American Kennel Club, or any other dog registry for that matter, has a written description called the "standard." This portrays the perfect dog of that breed, describing every aspect in detail. The standard is written by peo-

ple with expert knowledge of the breed, usually a club or committee composed of long-time breeders, exhibitors and judges.

When a dog competes in a dog show, it is judged not only against the other dogs of its breed competing that day, but also against the written standard. The dog that wins is the dog that most closely compares with the written description, as compared to the other dogs competing. The standard is also used to choose dogs for breeding. Breeders use the standard as a tool to see which dogs or bitches should pass on their genes to future generations.

Excerpts from the German Shepherd Dog standard, as approved by the American Kennel Club, are given in the following pages, with comments. The complete standard can be acquired from the American Kennel Club, whose address is in Chapter 13.

General Appearance

The Standard The first impression of a good German Shepherd Dog is that of a strong, agile, well-muscled animal, alert and full of life. It is well balanced, with harmonious development of the forequarter and hindquarter. The dog is longer than tall, deep-bodied and presents an outline of smooth curves rather than angles. He looks substantial and not spindly, giving the impression, both at rest and at motion, of muscular fitness and nimbleness without any look of clumsiness or soft living. The ideal dog is stamped with a look of quality and nobility—difficult to define, but unmistakable when present. Secondary sex characteristics are strongly marked, and every animal gives a definite impression of masculinity or femininity, according to its sex.

Comments When judging the appearance of a German Shepherd Dog, there are three things to look for. The first relates to the dog's overall appearance: The dog should be strong, agile, well muscled and nimble. German Shepherds are meant to work, and the dog should look capable of doing so.

WHAT IS A BREED STANDARD?

A breed standard—a detailed description of an individual breed—is meant to portray the *ideal* specimen of that breed. This includes ideal structure, temperament, gait, type—all aspects of the dog. Because the standard describes an ideal specimen, it isn't based on any particular dog. It is a concept against which judges compare actual dogs and breeders strive to produce dogs. At a dog show, the dog that wins is the one that comes closest, in the judge's opinion, to the standard for its breed. Breed standards are written by the breed parent clubs, the national organizations formed to oversee the well-being of the breed. They are voted on and approved by the members of the parent clubs.

Next comes the dog's expression. Each dog should be aware of the world around it: alert. The word "nobility" is also used to describe the German Shepherd and is synonymous with the breed's intelligence and character, as well as its impressive physical bearing. A German Shepherd's expression is hard to define but is easily recognized: the "look of eagles," some people have said.

Third, you should look for a clear difference between the sexes. A male German Shepherd Dog should look distinctly masculine and the bitch, feminine.

Character

Standard The breed has a distinct personality marked by a direct and fearless, but not hostile, expression, self-confidence and a certain aloofness that does not lend itself to immediate and indiscriminate friendships. The dog must be approachable, quietly standing his ground and showing confidence and willing-

The GSD's expression has been described as "the look of eagles."

ness to meet overtures without itself making them. It is poised, but when occasion demands, eager and alert; both fit and willing to serve in its capacity as companion, watchdog, blind leader, herding dog or guardian, whichever the circumstances may demand. The dog must not be timid, shrinking behind its master or handler; it should not be nervous, looking about or upward with anxious expression or showing nervous reactions, such as tucking of tail, to strange sights or sounds. Lack of confidence under any surroundings is not typical of good character.

Comments This paragraph is very detailed and self-explanatory; however, its importance cannot be stressed enough. Unfortunately, many German Shepherds do not have the correct temperament or character. Highly excitable, nervous, fearful, shy, timid or overly aggressive dogs cannot do the work the breed was designed to do. In addition, such dogs can be a danger to themselves, to their owners and to the public.

A German Shepherd with correct character is a dog willing to work with his owner, a dog to be respected for his dignity and intelligence.

Breeder Margie Jones got her first German Shepherd Dog in 1971 and says that she still loves the breed because of the dogs' character and personality. "I grew up seven miles from the Seeing Eye Guide Dog School and watched them training the German Shepherds. I fell in love with the dogs' intelligence, character, courage, nobility, loyalty and of course, their beauty. There is absolutely no other dog like a German Shepherd."

White GSDs exist but are disqualified in the show ring.

Head

Standard The head is noble, cleanly chiseled, strong without coarseness, but above all not fine, and in proportion to the body. The head of the male is distinctively masculine, and that of the bitch distinctly feminine. The muzzle is long and strong with lips firmly fitted, and the topline is parallel to the topline of the skull. Seen from the front, the forehead is only moderately arched, and the skull slopes into the long, wedge-shaped muzzle without an abrupt stop. Jaws are strongly developed.

Comments A proper German Shepherd's head is unmistakable. Even when shown alone in photographs or artwork, the head is easily recognized and conveys the aristocracy, personality and intelligence of the dog.

Ears

Standard Ears are moderately pointed, in proportion to the skull, open toward the front, and carried erect when at attention, the ideal carriage being one in which the center lines of the ears, viewed from the front, are parallel to each other and perpendicular to the ground. A dog with cropped or hanging ears must be disqualified.

Comments Like the head, the erect ears are another hallmark of the breed. Although other breeds have erect ears, none are like the German Shepherd's. Hanging, drooping, dropped or other incorrect ears detract from the overall appearance of the dog.

Eyes

Standard Of medium size, almond shaped, set a little obliquely, and not protruding. The color is as dark as possible. The expression is keen, intelligent and composed.

Comments Whoever penned the adage, "The eyes are the mirror of the soul," obviously owned dogs!

Teeth

Standard Forty-two in number—twenty upper and twenty-two lower, are strongly developed and meet in a scissors bite.

Comments A German Shepherd's teeth can affect many areas of his daily life, from the shape of his muzzle and head, to how he eats his food, to his ability to grip a steer he needs to herd or his ability to bite a criminal he's apprehending.

A proper GSD head is unmistakable.

Neck

Standard The neck is strong and muscular, clean-cut and relatively long, proportionate in size to the head and without loose folds of skin. When the dog is at attention or excited, the head is raised and the neck carried high; otherwise, typical carriage of the head is forward rather than up and only a little higher than the top of the shoulders, particularly in motion.

Comments A long neck carrying the head somewhat forward can greatly aid a dog's movement. Long neck muscles aid the shoulders, which help forward movement. A short neck can be unattractive and can also be symptomatic of poor shoulder conformation.

Forequarters

Standard The shoulder blades are long and obliquely angled, laid on flat and not placed forward. The upper arm joins the shoulder blade at about a right angle. Both the upper arm and shoulder blade are well muscled. The forelegs, viewed from all sides, are straight and the bone oval rather than round. The pasterns are strong and springy and angulated at approximately a 25-degree angle from vertical.

Comments A dog lacking proper angulation in both the forequarters and hindquarters is less efficient while moving and is more prone to injuries. Proper angulation allows the dog to move with the effortless gait that is typical of the breed.

THE AMERICAN KENNEL CLUB

Familiarly referred to as "the AKC," the American Kennel Club is a nonprofit organization devoted to the advancement of pure-bred dogs. The AKC maintains a registry of recognized breeds and adopts and enforces rules for dog events including shows, obedience trials, field trials, hunting tests, lure coursing, herding, earthdog trials, agility and the Canine Good Citizen program. It is a club of clubs, established in 1884 and composed, today, of over 500 autonomous dog clubs throughout the United States. Each club is represented by a delegate; the delegates make up the legislative body of the AKC, voting on rules and electing directors. The American Kennel Club maintains the Stud Book, the record of every dog ever registered with the AKC, and publishes a variety of materials on purebred dogs, including a monthly magazine, books and numerous educational pamphlets. For more information, contact the AKC at the address listed in Chapter 13, "Resources," and look for the names of their publications in Chapter 12, "Recommended Reading."

Feet

Standard The feet are short, compact, with toes well arched, pads thick and firm, nails short and dark.

Comments Solid feet with thick pads work as shock absorbers and snow tires; the feet cushion the shock of contact to the ground and they grip the ground. A dog with splayed feet, weak toes or thin pads will get foot-sore and be unable to work.

Proportion

Standard The German Shepherd Dog is longer than tall, with the most desirable proportion as 10 to $8\frac{1}{2}$. The desired height for males at the top of the highest point of the shoulder blade is 24 to 26 inches; for bitches, it's 22 to 24 inches. The length is measured from the point of the prosternum (or breast bone) to the rear edge of the pelvis, the ischial tuberosity.

The GSD should appear to be longer than it is tall.

Comments An easier way to visualize the proportion of the German Shepherd is to compare it to other breeds. A Basset Hound is obviously much longer than tall, as is a Dachshund. The Doberman Pinscher, on the other hand, should appear to be a square, with the height at the withers equalling the distance horizontally from the forechest to the farthest point of the upper thigh. The German Shepherd should appear to be longer than tall, but not extremely so.

Body

Standard The whole structure of the body gives an impression of depth and solidity without bulkiness.

11

Chest: Commencing at the prosternum, it is well filled and carried well down between the legs. It is deep and capacious, never shallow, with ample room for lungs and heart, carried well forward, with the prosternum showing ahead of the shoulder in profile. *Ribs:* Well sprung and long, they are neither barrel-shaped nor too flat, and are carried down to a sternum that reaches the elbows. Correct ribbing allows the elbows to move back freely when the dog is at a trot. Too round causes interference and throws the elbows out; too flat or short causes pinched elbows. Ribbing is carried well back so the loin is relatively short. *Abdomen:* Firmly held and not paunchy. The bottom line is only moderately tucked up in loin.

Comments This paragraph, when read slowly and carefully, is self-explanatory. If you have trouble visualizing it, run your hands over your dog as you do so, or compare the statements with the illustration.

Topline

Standard *Withers:* The withers are higher than and sloping into the level back. *Back:* The back is straight, very strongly developed without sag or roach, and relatively short. The desirable long proportion is not derived from a long back but from overall length of withers and hindquarters, viewed from the side. *Croup:* Long and gradually sloping. *Tail:* Bushy, with the last vertebra extended at least to the hock joint. It is set smoothly into the croup and low rather than high.

Comments This paragraph works together with the section describing the German Shepherd's correct proportions. The length of the shoulder blade and the length of the pelvis should be approximately the same. The pelvis should be sloped from the level back at a 30-degree angle. This, combined with correct shoulder angulation and sloping withers, provides for the look of a long back that the standard desires.

Hindquarters

Standard The whole assembly of the thigh, viewed from the side, is broad, with both upper and lower thigh well muscled, forming as nearly as possible a right angle.

Comments The hindquarter provides the power for the dog to move forward, much like a rear-wheel-driven car or a person pushing a grocery cart. Without the correct conformation, both in the hindquarters itself, but also in the back and the forequarters, power is decreased or lost.

Gait

Standard A German Shepherd is a trotting dog, and its structure has been developed to meet the requirements of its work. General impression: The gait is outreaching, elastic, seemingly without effort, smooth and rhythmic, covering the maximum amount of ground with the minimum number of steps. At a trot the dog moves powerfully but easily, with coordination and balance, so that the gait appears to be the steady motion of a well-lubricated machine.

The GSD's hindquarters give him the power to move forward.

Comments The trotting gait of a good German Shepherd is wonderful to watch; it's almost mystical. The dog seems to be moving without any effort at all and to be able to continue all day without fatigue.

Color

Standard The German Shepherd varies in color, and most colors are permissible. Strong, rich colors are preferred. Nose black. Pale, washed-out colors and blues or livers are serious faults. A white dog or a dog with a nose that is not predominantly black must be disqualified.

Comments The most commonly seen colors are black and tan, black and red, black and silver, sable and black. The black on the dog's back can range from a saddle to a complete cape. Black dogs may be entirely black or may have scattered tan, brown or gray hairs.

Although white German Shepherds have been mentioned throughout the breed's history, they are disqualified under the standard and are not desired.

Coat
Standard The ideal dog has a double coat of medium length. The outer coat should be as dense as possible, hair straight, harsh and lying close to the body. A slightly wavy outer coat, often of wiry texture, is permissible. The head, including the inner ear and foreface, and the legs and paws are covered with short hair, and the neck with longer, thicker hair. The rear of the forelegs and hindlegs has somewhat longer hair.

The German Shepherd Dog's Ancestry

Early History

The First Working Dogs

Most researchers think that dogs have been a part of mankind's history for at least 12,000 years. Cave drawings, grave sites and other archeological finds seem to support this time frame. What researchers don't agree on is exactly what the first dogs might have been. Were they wolves or the early ances-

A U.S. Grand Champion of 1922, Int. Ch. Hamilton v Grafenwerth, PH.

tors of wolves? Or were they a close relative—that evolved into dogs—that no longer exists in its former form? The first canine companion may have been a wolf drawn to a cave by meat scraps or an orphaned cub raised by a child or a lonely hunter. Perhaps it's good that we don't know, because it leaves room for the imagination.

*Roland v
Starkenburg,
German Grand
Champion for
1906 and '07.
Almost all
American GSDs
can trace back
to him.*

The first occupation of the early dogs was to guard the family's cave, warning of predators or trespassers. Dogs most certainly helped on the hunt for food and, as mankind domesticated other animals, dogs were used to protect and care for the family's livestock. Over thousands of years, herding dogs of various types were developed all over the world. There were long-coated, corded Pulis in Hungary, silky-coated Border Collies in Great Britain, massive Bouviers des Flandres in Belgium, and a variety of other breeds of all sizes, shapes, temperaments and coat types; the dogs were bred to work in a variety of terrains and climates, herding sheep, cattle, goats or ducks. Herding dogs became critical to mankind's survival.

In Germany, throughout history, herding dogs were selected for use by their ability to work. Dogs selected for breeding were chosen for their herding or guarding usefulness rather than their beauty. Therefore, there was no consistency of type, and certainly no one breed, used for herding.

The First German Shepherds Max von Stephanitz was born in Germany in 1864 to a family of some nobility. As a young adult, he entered the cavalry and in 1898 was promoted to captain, although shortly afterwards he was asked to leave the service when there was a scandal concerning his new wife, who was said to be an actress. Captain von Stephanitz had been interested in breeding dogs for many years and his discharge from the military gave him the time to continue that work.

The Captain was particularly interested in the sheep herding dogs found in Germany, as they were the true working dogs of that era. These dogs varied in size, build and type but were uniformly intelligent and predisposed to work. In 1899, Captain von Stephanitz attended a dog show and bought a working shepherd-type dog named Hektor Linkrsheim. Shortly thereafter he changed the dog's name to Horand von Grafarth. Horand was a large dog, 24 inches tall, with good bone and clean lines. He was athletic, strong and full of life. Photographs of him show the distinctive German Shepherd head, ears and expression.

That same year, Captain von Stephanitz and his friend Artur Meyer founded the Verein für Deutsche Shäferhunde (SV), or Club for German Shepherds, and Horand became the first registered German Shepherd Dog. The club sponsored a dog show for the new breed each year beginning in 1899, and Captain von Stephanitz judged each event. The top dog (male) was awarded the title *Sieger,* and the top bitch (female), *Siegerin.* By judging these shows, the Captain was able to guide the breed's development and he became an expert at analyzing pedigrees for dogs' flaws and virtues. Under Captain von Stephanitz's guidance, the German Shepherd emerged as a purebred dog of supreme intelligence, nobility and usefulness: a sound mind in a sound body.

Since the breed's intelligence and usefulness were of utmost importance, the Captain began obedience contests and herding trials. Training trials were started with awards to outstanding dogs. He also introduced the dogs to police officers, who welcomed the dogs after finding how useful they were in apprehending criminals.

WHERE DID DOGS COME FROM?

It can be argued that dogs were right there at man's side from the beginning of time. As soon as human beings began to document their existence, the dog was among their drawings and inscriptions. Dogs were not just friends, they served a purpose: There were dogs to hunt birds, pull sleds, herd sheep, burrow after rats—even sit in laps! What your dog was originally bred to do influences the way it behaves. The American Kennel Club recognizes over 140 breeds, and there are hundreds more distinct breeds around the world. To make sense of the breeds, they are grouped according to their size or function. The AKC has seven groups:

1) Sporting, 2) Working,
3) Herding, 4) Hounds,
5) Terriers, 6) Toys,
7) Nonsporting

Can you name a breed from each group? Here's some help: (1) Golden Retriever; (2) Doberman Pinscher; (3) Collie; (4) Beagle; (5) Scottish Terrier; (6) Maltese; and (7) Dalmatian. All modern domestic dogs (*Canis familiaris*) are related, however different they look, and are all descended from *Canis lupus,* the gray wolf.

World War I introduced Captain von Stephanitz's dogs to the world. German Shepherds served as messenger dogs, worked as guard and sentry dogs and alerted their handlers to the presence of enemy soldiers. It was the breed's work with the Red Cross that earned the dogs international acclaim, however. Numerous dogs searched for wounded soldiers and led Red Cross workers to them, saving thousands of lives.

Tommy, the German Shepherd mascot of a Scottish regiment, was wounded in action at least three times, was captured and later rescued, and was gassed by the enemy. At the war's end, Tommy received the Croix de Guerre medal for gallantry.

By 1923, the membership of Captain von Stephanitz's Club for German Shepherds had grown to 57,000. Unfortunately, the Nazi rise to power and Adolf Hitler's interest in the breed were the Captain's undo-

A 1958 photo
of Ch. Hero von
Aichtal of
Giralda.

ing. Hitler's favorite German Shepherd was Blondie, given to him by Martin Bormann in 1941. Blondie flew with Hitler in his FW-200 Condor and died with him in a bunker during the Allied invasion.

Captain von Stephanitz died in 1936 after the Nazis had taken the Club for German Shepherds away from him by threatening him with internment in a concentration camp. However, his memory lives on in a breed of dog renowned for its beauty, loyalty, nobility, intelligence, temperament and strong working instincts.

The Evolving German Shepherd

Around the World The German Shepherd's working abilities spread around the world during and after World War I. European countries imported the breed in great numbers and quickly put it to work. African and South American countries, Japan and other Far East countries also imported numerous amounts.

In France, the national club is called La Société du Chien Berger Siegerschau, and sponsors an annual show in Vichy, often judged by a judge from the German SV club. Today the breed is commonly used by guards and customs agents, especially in the mountainous areas of the country. German Shepherds are used to track criminals, search for avalanche victims or catch smugglers.

Belgium, Holland and Sweden all use working German Shepherds and import dogs from Germany as well as breed their own. Sweden has a corps of German Shepherds trained for avalanche search-and-rescue work that has been used as an example for search-and-rescue groups around the world. The dogs are transported by helicopter to avalanche sites, where they use their keen sense of smell to find buried victims.

Switzerland has a large number of working dogs in its police force; in fact, the ratio is one dog per every three policemen. Beginning in World War II, the German Shepherd found its niche serving as a messenger, a guard and protector, a search-and-rescue dog and a police dog.

Swiss dog fanciers have carried on Captain von Stephanitz's desire to screen dog breeding in order to preserve the quality of the breed. Before a dog is bred, it must pass a conformation test where it is judged against the breed standard. The dog is then given a temperament test, which includes the dog's responses to different situations, including friendly strangers, a noisy crowd of people and being left alone. The dog must also navigate an obstacle course, which includes things to go over, under and through. In addition, visual and sound stimuli—including gunfire— test the dog's reactions.

On to the United States. American soldiers returned to the United States after World War I with tales of these wonderful dogs. Rin Tin Tin and Strongheart popularized the breed even more, and everyone wanted a

German Shepherd. Unfortunately, unscrupulous breeders produced a number of unsound dogs with poor temperaments and by the late 1920s, the breed suffered a decline in popularity.

However, serious breeders continued to import good quality dogs from Germany, including the 1937 *Sieger* Pfeffer von Bern, who went on to win in United States dog shows as well, becoming the 1937 and 1938 U.S. Grand Victor. Utilizing these imported dogs and carefully following Captain von Stephanitz's guidelines for breeding, breeders reestablished the German Shepherd in the United States. The first German Shepherd recognized by the American Kennel Club was Queen of Switzerland, a bitch imported from Germany. She was registered in 1908.

The breed went through another popularity surge and subsequent decline after World War II, for much the same reasons, and again serious breeders tried to bring the breed back to an even keel. They succeeded. By 1993, German Shepherds were third in popularity in American Kennel Club registrations, just behind Labrador Retrievers and Rottweilers, with over 79,000 dogs registered during the year.

GSDs are versatile workers.

The German Shepherd Dog Club of America today is a large, powerful club with chapters all over the country. Local and regional clubs host shows all year round and the national club sponsors the National Show each year, with the winning dog and bitch named the Grand Victor and Grand Victrix. The clubs also emphasize the working abilities of the breed, hosting shows for obedience, tracking, herding and Schutzhund, a sport that combines obedience, tracking, and protection work.

The German Shepherd serves in many occupations in the United States, more so than any other breed. In fact, the breed's work in the United States has earned it the title of the greatest service dog in existence.

Working Dog Extraordinaire

Law Enforcement German Shepherds have served and continue to serve in police departments all over the United States and the world. The famous Scotland Yard police force in Britain in the 1950s kept a large corps of well-trained German Shepherds. Top canine cops today are often honored for their contributions with dinners, medals and articles in local newspapers. The best measure of law enforcement canines is the undisputed fact that criminals and underworld figures have offered rewards for the killing of certain particularly effective police dogs.

Law enforcement dogs search for lost people and escaping criminals, sniff for drugs or other contraband and are taught to protect their handlers and other officers at all costs. Many courageous and loyal dogs have died serving their handlers.

Just the sight of a police dog can be effective. John Hammond and his German Shepherd, Ajax, serve in Ocean City, California. "The city hosts a summer festival each year and it attracts a number of teenagers from all over," he says. "Sometimes the parties get rowdy. But when Ajax and I show up on the scene, you can hear the word spread. 'Cool it, man, the dog is here!' . . . It's great!"

Military Dogs have been used by the military since the Roman invasion of Europe. The Romans used dogs extensively, for herding, as beasts of burden and as part of their fighting forces. In retaliation, the Germans learned how to train their dogs, too, and in some battles, dogs were used on both sides. In the late 1700s, Napoleon Bonaparte urged his generals to use sentry dogs.

Today, the military uses dogs in many of the same capacities as law enforcement departments, except that many military dogs are also taught to search for weapons or explosives. Military German Shepherds have served on bases in the United States as well as overseas, aboard ship and in aircraft. Some have even learned to parachute, strapped to their handlers in specially designed harnesses.

Search and Rescue The German Shepherd's strong working instincts, intelligence and wonderful scenting abilities have made it a premier search-and-rescue dog. Trained dogs and their owners have found lost hikers and campers, children who have wandered away and the elderly who might be confused and lost. German Shepherds have worked in earthquake rubble in Mexico City, San Francisco, Los Angeles and Armenia, saving countless lives.

The GSD is an infamous law-enforcement dog.

After the 1994 earthquake in Los Angeles, the Metropolitan K9 Platoon brought in six German Shepherd Dogs to search a collapsed apartment building. The dogs searched more than one hundred apartments that had been reduced to rubble and found numerous survivors and bodies. During their search, aftershocks continued to shake the unstable building.

Search-and-rescue German Shepherds have worked to find flood victims and people swept away by mudslides and avalanches. Although St. Bernards are the most famous search-and-rescue dogs of Switzerland and the Alps, there are actually many more German Shepherds working than there are St. Bernards.

Schutzhund The sport of Schutzhund was designed to test the working abilities of German working dogs, German Shepherds in particular. Schutzhund consists of three parts: obedience, tracking and protection work, and the dog must be proficient in all three areas.

Schutzhund competition was founded by the German Working Dog Federation, of which the SV club is a member. In the United States, the German Shepherd Dog Club of America Working Dog Association is the primary club for German Shepherds, although several other organizations also sponsor Schutzhund trials.

Guide Dogs A German king in 100 B.C. was reportedly the first to use guide dogs. Another guide dog, shown leading a blind man, was depicted by an artist on the wall of a house in Pompeii, buried for centuries by the volcanic eruption in A.D. 79. Modern-day guide dogs were first trained in France. Buddy, a German Shepherd bitch, was, in 1927, the first Seeing Eye dog in the United States. Today, there are several guide dog schools all over the country, and although other breeds are also used, German Shepherds are still the breed of choice.

Movies and Television The most famous German Shepherd of all time and the dog most responsible for the popularity of German Shepherds was born in the trenches, under fire in World War I. Rin Tin Tin, an extremely intelligent dog, didn't have the proper conformation to be a competitive show dog. But under the training of Lee Duncan, the dog made over forty movies between 1923 and his death in 1932. Rin Tin Tin's movies made millions and saved his studio, Warner Brothers, from bankruptcy while at the same time making him the biggest and most popular dog star of all time.

More recently, in the movie *K–9,* a handsome German Shepherd plays a police dog paired with a human police officer who doesn't quite know what to make of his canine partner. The movie is a wonderful demonstration of the trainability of the breed.

And More The breed's intelligence, physical abilities and love of work have made German Shepherds useful in many different occupations. They have used their scenting abilities to find truffles, a fungus that many regard as a delicacy. Their exceptional sense of smell

**FAMOUS
OWNERS OF
GERMAN
SHEPHERD
DOGS**

Franklin
Delano
Roosevelt

Sigmund
Freud

George
Hamilton

Bob Hope

Jack LaLanne

Roy Rogers

23

has enabled them to sniff out underground gas leaks in city pipes or find termites secreted in walls.

German Shepherds pull wagons, herd cattle or sheep, serve as watchdogs or guard dogs, alert the hearing disabled to sounds or dangers and much, much more. The German Shepherd is, without a doubt, a service dog *extraordinaire.*

Elizabeth Stidham, a German Shepherd breeder whose dogs compete in conformation, obedience and tracking competitions, said in the American Kennel *Gazette* magazine, "Not only is the German Shepherd Dog one of the world's most popular breeds, but it is also the breed of choice of most working dog handlers and of service organizations that use dogs. A German Shepherd possessing the physical and psychological attributes called for in the breed standard is an incomparable canine assistant. No other breed has served humanity in more ways than the German Shepherd Dog."

The Ultimate Companion Dog

Famous Dogs The breed's popularity with Europeans and Americans has been reflected in its ownership by celebrities in all walks of life.

President Franklin Delano Roosevelt had two German Shepherds, Major and Meg, both of whom had reputations for using their teeth too freely. Major bit Senator Hattie Caraway and England's Prime Minister James MacDonald, while Meg bit journalist Bess Furman.

Sigmund Freud, the psychoanalyst, was a dog lover who owned a German Shepherd called Wolf. One day in Vienna, Wolf was lost, and although the family searched in vain he could not be found. Later that same day, the dog showed up in a taxi. The dog had jumped in and refused to move until the driver read his name and address on his collar tags. When the taxi pulled up in front of his home, the dog jumped out.

Family Dogs Although the popularity of German Shepherds began with their work with the Red Cross,

Seeing Eye and military and through Rin Tin Tin's visibility in the movies, the breed has remained popular because of its extreme loyalty toward its people. German Shepherds are devoted, responsible, loyal dogs—sometimes to a fault—and will literally give their lives for their owners.

Joe Karas, a member of the National Association of Dog Obedience Instructors who teaches dog obedience classes and competes in obedience and Schutzhund, calls the German Shepherd "more than a dog." He said, "I was attracted to the breed by its appearance but also the feeling that this dog would be a totally devoted companion, loyal to me and my family, and I found that in Major. He was an excellent, alert dog, a laid-back pal and was wonderful with my two kids." Karas added, "Major died in 1992, but I still love him."

The GSD is a totally devoted companion.

Marion Schular, who also competes with her dogs in conformation and obedience as well as tracking, got her first German Shepherd in the 1950s and said, "All my life I have loved this breed. I love its beauty, its loyalty, intelligence and temperament—the Rin Tin Tin qualities!"

Elizabeth Stidham said, "The loyalty of the German Shepherd is legendary; the depth of its bond to its handler is well documented. Coupling courage with calm confidence, independence with compliance, derring-do with dignity, provides the balance that makes the German Shepherd Dog the world's premier working dog."

chapter 3

The **World**

According to the **German Shepherd Dog**

Ancestry

Herding Instincts German Shepherd Dogs are descended from herding dogs and are even today classified by the American Kennel Club as a herding breed. A few, but not many, German Shepherds herd sheep or cattle in the United States today, although many German Shepherds still herd sheep and cattle in Europe. However, the instincts that make a dog a good herding dog can still be seen in many German Shepherds, even those that have never met a sheep.

The herding instincts, chase instincts and prey drive are very close. In fact, an overenthusiastic or unsupervised herding dog of any breed can become a stock killer. This prey drive or chase instinct can

Welcome to
the World of
the German
Shepherd Dog

cause a dog to chase anything that moves: sheep, cattle, cats, cars or children. Naturally, this can be a good talent when used properly in a working herding dog, but it can cause major problems when the dog chases cars or children or kills livestock.

Herding dogs can show their talents in a variety of ways, one of which is by nipping at heels, as they would do to get cattle moving. Obviously, this is undesirable in a companion dog. Another herding instinct is that of circling. With sheep or cattle, the dog would run a circle or boundary around the flock or herd to keep it in a specific area, perhaps to keep it out of a field or off the street. Again, this is wonderful for a dog herding sheep but can be extremely annoying when the dog won't allow the kids to leave a ten-foot circle the dog has arbitrarily set up as a boundary!

Although herding instincts are very strong, they can be controlled—by teaching the dog what is allowed and what isn't, and by letting the dog use its instincts constructively. If the kids get angry when the dog keeps them herded into a small circle, teach the dog what the real boundaries are. Many a toddler has been prevented from wandering away by an alert German Shepherd or other attentive herding dog.

Protective Instincts The German Shepherd's instincts to guard his property come from both his herding instincts and his use as a guard dog and watchdog. A good herding dog must be able to guard his flock

A DOG'S SENSES

Sight: With their eyes located farther apart than ours, dogs can detect movement at a greater distance than we can, but they can't see as well up close. They can also see better in less light, but can't distinguish many colors.

Sound: Dogs can hear about four times better than we can, and they can hear high-pitched sounds especially well. Their ancestors, the wolves, howled to let other wolves know where they were; our dogs do the same, but they have a wider range of vocalizations, including barks, whimpers, moans and whines.

Smell: A dog's nose is his greatest sensory organ. His sense of smell is so great he can follow a trail that's weeks old, detect odors diluted to one-millionth the concentration we'd need to notice them, even sniff out a person under water!

Taste: Dogs have fewer taste buds than we do, so they're likelier to try anything—and usually do, which is why it's especially important for their owners to monitor their food intake. Dogs are omnivores, which means they eat meat as well as vegetable matter like grasses and weeds.

Touch: Dogs are social animals and love to be petted, groomed and played with.

from predators and trespassers. When there is no flock to protect, the German Shepherd protects his people and their property. This protective instinct can be seen every day: in the dog's active barking when people approach the house and low growling when a stranger approaches the family children.

This protective instinct, combined with her herding instincts and her desire to work, which we will discuss later, is what makes the breed so valuable to the police and military.

Because of this instinct, many people view German Shepherds as standoffish or aloof, as well they should. German Shepherds do not greet every person they meet with a wagging tail and a licking tongue; other dogs can do that. Instead, German Shepherds will stand their ground and look people in the eye. Friendly strangers may be greeted with a slightly wagging tail. Strange or threatening people will be greeted with a growl.

However, this doesn't mean the breed is cold or unfeeling. Known friends will be remembered, recognized and greeted as friends. Depending upon the dog and how good a friend you are, the greeting may be a cold nose in the palm of the hand and a wagging tail or it may be a frenzied greeting that includes a dancing body, a licking tongue and cries of joy.

The GSD is a multitalented athlete.

Drive to Work No, the German Shepherd doesn't need a car to drive; however, she does need a job. Because the breed was derived from herding dogs and was designed to work, German Shepherds need an occupation, something to keep the mind challenged and the body busy.

A bored German Shepherd will become a bad German Shepherd, guaranteed. Many bored German Shepherds start running the fence in their yard, back and forth, back and forth, just as a tiger in a cage that is too small might do. Or the bored dog might start barking, digging up the backyard, chewing up the couch or the lawn furniture, or he may even start chewing on himself.

Shepherds will not go unnoticed in your home.

There are quite a few different jobs you can give your German Shepherd. Use the dog's obedience training to give her some structure in her life and to teach her to work for you, to listen to your commands. Teach her to bring you your newspaper and to find your slippers or keys. Teach her to find your kids by name. Find someone in your area who gives herding lessons and enroll in a class. Let your dog use those instincts. Find a dog training club in your area and try something new, like agility, flyball or scent hurdle races. Teach your dog to play frisbee. All of these things will keep your German Shepherd busy, focused and happy. (For more on these activities, see Part III, "Enjoying Your Dog.")

Living with a German Shepherd

Size The German Shepherd is considered a medium- to large-sized dog, averaging from 60 to 100 pounds when full grown. That means a 60- to 100-pound dog stretched out across the living-room floor or curled up on the sofa. A dog this large does not go unnoticed in a household, and many times adjustments need to be made.

However, a German Shepherd's heart is not medium size, it's huge, and everything this breed does, it does in a big way. When a German Shepherd loves you, he loves you totally and completely. When a German Shepherd guides his blind owner, protects his law-enforcement partner, accepts obedience training, sleeps on your sofa or even just chews on a rawhide, he does so totally, thoroughly and completely.

Strength The German Shepherd is a powerful dog and without training could easily jump on and knock down a child, a senior citizen or even an unprepared adult. After all, in law enforcement work, the breed is expected to be able to overpower criminals. However, with training, the dog can learn to restrain that power, using it only when it is required.

Senses As with most dogs, the senses of smell and hearing are the most important senses to the German Shepherd. Sight, touch and taste are used, but not to the extent that hearing and smell are.

Your GSD loves to work for you and be with you.

The German Shepherd's sense of smell is so acute, we can barely comprehend it. Dogs taught to use their sense of smell as an occupation, such as narcotic detection dogs, can distinguish between two 20-gallon tubs of water, one of which has one teaspoon of salt dissolved in it. Considering we find salt to be almost completely odorless, this ability is simply amazing. This wonderful sense of smell has allowed German Shepherds to serve humans in many ways. They can detect narcotics, contraband food, explosives, termites, gas leaks, water leaks and, of course, people.

Because this sense is so acute, many German Shepherds spend quite a bit of time smelling the grass, sniffing fence posts and bushes or simply inhaling the breeze. Each inhale of breath brings the dog messages from the world around her that we are unaware of; and it can be frustrating sometimes. Exactly what is the dog smelling? What is so fascinating? If only she could tell us!

German Shepherds can also hear better than we can. Their frequency range extends higher than ours and they can hear much fainter sounds. Another ability that surpasses ours is the ability to find the origin of sounds: Those large erect ears work almost like radar detectors, allowing the dog to pinpoint exactly where the sound came from.

Many German Shepherd owners get angry because their dog will, with no apparent reason, start barking.

CHARACTERISTICS OF A GERMAN SHEPHERD DOG

Strong herding instinct

Protectiveness

Acute senses of hearing and smell

Requires daily strenuous exercise

Sheds, especially in spring and fall

Easily housetrained

The reason may not have been apparent to us, but the dog obviously heard something. I had a personal experience where I should have listened to my dogs but I didn't. Late one evening, my two German Shepherds, Watachie and Michi, began acting restless and kept looking out the sliding glass doors to the backyard. I turned on the light but didn't see anything, so I told the dogs to be quiet and go lie down. They did so, but continued to growl. A few minutes later, they both erupted in furious barks as only a German Shepherd can do. Again, I checked outside but again saw nothing. I yelled at the dogs and again made them lie down. The next day I found out my neighbor's house had been burglarized. If I had paid more attention, I could have called the police and perhaps the burglars would have been caught. My dogs knew much better than I that something strange was going on.

Experts used to think dogs saw only in black and white. Recently, however, researchers tested several dogs using a computer and found that dogs can see color; not the range of colors that most people see, but instead a limited range of colors, much like a color-blind person. It turned out that up to this point, we simply didn't know how to ask the dogs what they saw. Understanding that dogs can see color opens up an

entirely new vista in our understanding of dogs, and research is continuing to discover exactly how well they can see.

Activity Level The German Shepherd is a fairly high-energy dog who requires daily

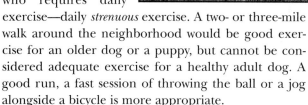

This German Shepherd Dog is intently herding ducks.

exercise—daily *strenuous* exercise. A two- or three-mile walk around the neighborhood would be good exercise for an older dog or a puppy, but cannot be considered adequate exercise for a healthy adult dog. A good run, a fast session of throwing the ball or a jog alongside a bicycle is more appropriate.

As mentioned earlier, the German Shepherd's drive to work can turn destructive if the dog doesn't have a job to do. The same thing can happen when the dog doesn't get enough exercise. Many German Shepherds will pace, run the fences, bark, chew or try to escape from the yard. However, you'll find that when your German Shepherd has been exercised daily, your dog will be healthier, happier and more relaxed, and destructiveness around the house and yard will be decreased.

Hair, Hair and More Hair! German Shepherds shed. There is no way to get around it. That wonderful, thick, weather-resistant coat does shed. If dog hair in the house bothers you, don't get a German Shepherd. German Shepherd owners all deal with the problem in different ways. Some vacuum daily, others buy carpet that matches the dog's coat, others pull up the carpet and put down tile. Living with a German Shepherd requires a few compromises, and understanding that the dog sheds is one of them.

The worst shedding times are spring and fall, depending upon the climate, but some shedding takes place all year round. The easiest way to keep it under control is to brush the dogs thoroughly every day. Chapter 6, Grooming Your German Shepherd Dog, will go into more detail, but it is important to mention shedding here because it does affect how you live with your dog.

Neat Other than shedding, German Shepherds are fairly neat dogs. Most housetrain very easily and, in fact, many will relieve themselves (of their own accord) in one corner of the yard. German Shepherds do not drool, and their personal habits are very clean. A well-trained, well-exercised dog will be a calm, quiet household companion, happy to lie by your feet as you read or watch television.

German Shepherd Guide Dogs

Most schools that train dogs to lead and assist the blind now use a few different breeds of dogs. Labrador Retrievers, Golden Retrievers, Doberman Pinschers and Australian Shepherds are commonly used and, on rare occasions, even Standard Poodles have been trained. For many schools, though, German Shepherds are still the breed of choice.

Many German Shepherds work as rescue dogs.

The reason for using different breeds varies. Sometimes it has been difficult for schools to find German Shepherds that were temperamentally and physically sound. Other times, it has been because the trainers needed the skills other breeds could offer.

Although every dog of every breed is different, some generalizations can be made about some of the dogs used for guide dog training. Most instructors agree that German Shepherds and Standard Poodles work faster than most Labs or Goldens. They walk faster, turn quicker and react more quickly. That means these dogs need to be paired with people who can work at this speed, such as a healthy, active person. People who walk more slowly or who have slower reactions would be better off with a Lab. Someone suffering with an illness might be better off with a soft, gentle Golden. An alert, responsible German Shepherd might be overwhelmed by life in the big city, whereas a calm, steady Golden might thrive on it. Although few children are paired with a guide dog, children and young teenagers are often better with a slightly smaller dog, like an Aussie.

Guide dog instructors use these generalizations as guidelines when selecting dogs to be admitted into the training program and when pairing up trained dogs and their future partners. Ultimately, the decision whether or not to use a dog is based upon the dog's physical and emotional soundness, its working drive and its responsibilities toward its handler, not its breed.

An Incredible Sense of Smell

On March 7, 1972, Brandy, a German Shepherd serving with New York City's bomb squad, responded to a call at La Guardia International Airport. A 707 had returned to the airport after takeoff when it received a telephone call reporting a bomb on board. When the aircraft touched down, the passengers were evacuated via the chutes at each side of the plane, and Brandy and her handler were let on board. Within seven seconds of boarding the plane, Brandy located a briefcase smuggled in as crew baggage. Examination by the bomb squad personnel showed the briefcase contained a time-bomb mechanism and $4\frac{1}{2}$ pounds of plastic explosives, enough to totally demolish the plane.

During her career, Brandy responded to over 1,000 calls and discovered over fifty explosive devices. To her credit, she never missed one.

MORE INFORMATION ON GERMAN SHEPHERD DOGS

NATIONAL BREED CLUB

German Shepherd Dog Club of America, Inc.
Blanche Beisswenger, Corresponding Secretary
17 West Ivy Lane
Englewood, NJ 07631

The club can send you information on the breed itself as well as the names and locations of local dog clubs or German Shepherd Dog clubs in your area. It can also provide information on obedience and herding clubs and other ways to get active with your German Shepherd Dog. Inquire about membership.

BOOKS

Antesberger, Helmut. *The German Shepherd Dog, a Complete Pet Owner's Manual.* Hauppauge, N.Y.: Barron's Educational Series, Inc., 1985.

Bennett, Jane. *The New Complete German Shepherd Dog.* New York: Howell Book House, 1987.

Lanting, Fred L. *The Total German Shepherd Dog.* Loveland, Colo.: Alpine Publications, 1990.

Nicholas, Anna Katherine. *The Book of the German Shepherd Dog.* Neptune, N.J.: TFH Publications, Inc., 1983.

Strickland, Winifred and Moses, James. *The German Shepherd Today, A Complete Reference for the German Shepherd Owner.* New York: Howell Book House, 1988.

Walkowicz, Chris. *The German Shepherd Dog.* Wilsonville, Ore.: Doral Publications, 1991

Willis, Malcolm B., Bsc, PhD. *The German Shepherd Dog, A Genetic History.* New York: Howell Book House, 1992.

Willis, Malcolm B., Bsc, PhD. *Pet Owner's Guide to the German Shepherd Dog*. New York: Howell Book House, 1993.

MAGAZINES

German Shepherd Dog Review, 30 Far View Rd., Chalfont, Pa. 18914.

German Shepherd Dog Quarterly, Hoflin Publishing, Inc., 4401 Zephyr St., Wheat Ridge, Colo. 80033–3299.

VIDEOS

American Kennel Club. *German Shepherd Dog*.

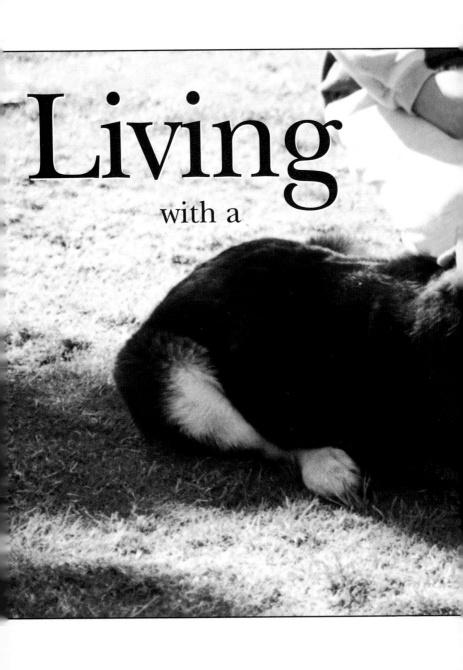

Living
with a

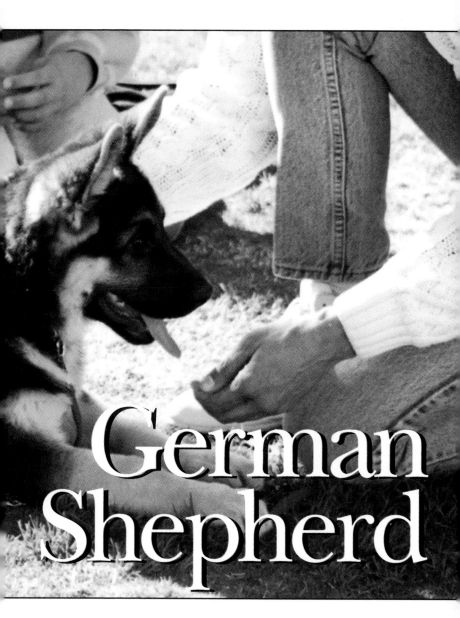

part two

German Shepherd

chapter 4

Bringing your
German
Shepherd Dog
Home

First Things First

Supplies Before you bring your German Shepherd home, you will need some supplies. You don't want to have to make an emergency run to the store at midnight because you forgot something. Some of the supplies are basic, for both the puppy and the adopted adult. Others are for one or the other.

Obviously, you will need dog food. Find out what the puppy is eating now and get some of that same food. If you wish to switch to a different brand, do so over a period of time so that your German Shepherd can adjust. Rapid changes of foods can result in an upset stomach and diarrhea.

You will need a bowl for food and a bowl for water. The food bowl can be just about anything; some people like plastic, others like ceramic or stainless steel. Whatever you use should be large enough to hold four to six cups of food and should be easily cleaned. Many people keep the dog's water bowl outside, since many German Shepherd puppies like to play and splash in their water. If you do keep the bowl outside, make sure it is large enough to hold two or three gallons of water and that it is unspillable. Change the water and clean the bowl daily, and if your German Shepherd likes to splash in it, check it a couple of times a day to make sure the dog doesn't go thirsty.

You will also need a collar and leash for your new German Shepherd. A buckle collar, either with a metal buckle or the plastic quick-release closure, is good for both puppies and adult dogs. Adjustable collars are available that can be made larger as the puppy grows.

When you start dog training classes with your German Shepherd, your instructor may ask that you use a different collar. There are many different types of training collars on the market, and your instructor can give you some guidance as to what might work better for you and your dog.

You will want an identification tag for your dog's buckle collar. This tag should include your name and both a daytime and an evening telephone number. You can order this tag prior to picking up your dog so you have it ready, or you can use one of the temporary tags available in many pet stores. With these tags, you write the information on a piece of paper, which is then sealed inside a plastic case. Later, when you have your dog and have chosen a name, you can order a new tag with your dog's name on it.

Your new German Shepherd will need a kennel crate to use as a bed, a place of refuge and a place for quiet time. This crate can be the plastic type that airlines require or it can be a heavy metal wire cage. The style

PUPPY ESSENTIALS

Your new puppy will need:

food bowl

water bowl

collar

leash

I.D. tag

bed

crate

toys

grooming supplies

is up to you, but the crate should be large enough for an adult German Shepherd to stand up, turn around and lie down in comfortably.

Last, but certainly not least, you will need some toys for your German Shepherd. If you are going to be bringing

Children and puppies just seem to go together.

home a new puppy, the toys should be something the puppy can chew on, because very shortly your puppy will start teething and will have a driving need to chew. Many dog owners like to offer rawhides (cured beef hide), while others like to give their dogs hard rubber toys to chew on. Again, it's your choice and, of course, what your dog prefers. Just make sure your puppy can't chew off and swallow small pieces of the toy.

If you are bringing home an older puppy or adult German Shepherd, you will have to offer larger rawhides or indestructible toys, as German Shepherds have incredibly strong jaws. Ask at your local pet store what they have available.

GETTING YOUR HOUSE READY

Prior to bringing home your German Shepherd, you will need to make sure your house is ready. First of all, set up the crate in your bedroom. Many people take away the nightstand next to the bed and put the crate right there. This way your dog will spend six to eight hours close to you and can smell and hear you all night long. This is a great way to bond with the dog, and you don't even have to do anything. Also, if the puppy needs to go outside during the night, you will hear the puppy whine and cry before there is an accident.

Next, decide where your dog will spend her days. If you are home all day, this is not a big problem; you can supervise the puppy when she's out and about. When you can't watch the pup, you can put her in her crate. However, if you work outside the home, you will need a secure place, preferably outside.

If you will be leaving your German Shepherd outside, you might want to build him a secure run or exercise area. Make sure your dog won't be able to climb or dig out of it and that other dogs, coyotes or predators can't get in. Your dog will need a house and shelter from the weather and an unspillable water bowl.

Next, you must make sure your house, yard and garage are safe for your new German Shepherd. It's amazing what an inquisitive puppy or bored adult dog can get into. In the house, crawl around on your hands and knees and look at things from a dog's viewpoint. Are there dangling electrical cords that might be fun to chew on? Are books or knickknacks within reach? Are VCR tapes stored at eye level? Pick up or put away anything that looks even remotely inter-

Puppies need their rest, too.

esting. Start teaching family members to close closet doors, pick up dirty clothes and put away shoes and slippers. With a young puppy or a new dog in the house, preventing problems from happening is imperative.

If your German Shepherd is going to have access to the garage, make sure all chemicals, paints and car parts are up high out of reach. Many things, like antifreeze, are very poisonous. You may even want to fence off part of the garage so there is absolutely no access to storage areas. Four-by-eight-foot framed wooden lattice is available at most lumber stores and makes great temporary dividers. By sectioning off the garage and picking up and storing away dangerous substances, you can ensure your dog's safety.

In the yard, look for possible escape routes, places where your dog could go under or over the fence. A pile of lumber or a rabbit hutch next to the fence could provide an easy escape route. A drainage ditch running under the fence could do the same thing. Again, just as in the house, try to look at your yard from the dog's point of view.

Also in the yard, put away garden tools, fertilizers, pesticides and pool supplies. If you have potted plants, pick them up before your German Shepherd turns them into play toys. Check the list of poisonous plants (see the sidebar, "Household Dangers") to make sure your land-scaping and potted plants are safe, just in case your dog does try to sample them.

A German Shepherd in the House

SETTING UP A SCHEDULE

Dogs are creatures of habit and thrive on a regular routine that doesn't vary too much from day to day. Baby puppies, especially, need a routine. At eight weeks of age, puppies sleep a lot. Your puppy will eat, relieve himself, play and sleep, and a couple of hours later will repeat the whole cycle. However, as he gets older, he will gradually sleep less and play more. As he learns and develops bowel and bladder control, he will go longer periods between needing to relieve himself, from every couple of hours to every three or four hours.

A sample schedule might look like this:

HOUSEHOLD DANGERS

Curious puppies and inquisitive dogs get into trouble not because they are bad, but simply because they want to investigate the world around them. It's our job to protect our dogs from harmful substances, like the following:

IN THE HOUSE

cleaners, especially pine oil

perfumes, colognes, aftershaves

medications, vitamins

office and craft supplies

electric cords

chicken or turkey bones

chocolate

some house and garden plants, like ivy, oleander and poinsettia

IN THE GARAGE

antifreeze

garden supplies, like snail and slug bait, pesticides, fertilizers, mouse and rat poisons

---

6:00 A.M. Dad gets up and goes outside with Puppy. Praises Puppy for relieving herself, then puts Puppy back in her crate.

7:00 A.M. Mom gets up, lets Puppy outside again, and gets Junior up to get ready for school. After Junior leaves for school, Mom feeds Puppy breakfast, plays with Puppy for a few minutes, then puts Puppy in her pen outside, giving Puppy a couple of chew toys. Mom leaves for work.

Noon. A neighbor comes over, lets Puppy out of the pen, plays with Puppy for a few minutes, and offers Puppy lunch. After Puppy has eaten and relieved herself, the neighbor sits down and cuddles Puppy for a few minutes, plays some more and then puts Puppy back in the pen.

You can start gently training your puppy right away.

3:00 P.M. Junior comes home from school and, after changing clothes, lets Puppy out of the pen. Junior lets Puppy relieve herself, then brings Puppy inside with him. They play, cuddle, and while Junior works on his homework, Puppy chews on a toy.

5:00 P.M. After finishing his homework, Junior takes Puppy for a walk.

6:00 P.M. Mom and Dad come home from work, and both greet Puppy. Junior takes Puppy outside to relieve herself.

7:00 P.M. After Puppy has eaten dinner and relieved herself, Dad gets down on the living-room floor with Puppy and grooms the pup, teaching the puppy to accept brushing, combing and nail trimming and, at the same time, checking her ears and so on. After grooming the puppy, Dad plays ball with the pup.

10:00 P.M. Dad takes Puppy outside to relieve herself and then crates the puppy for the night.

This is, of course, a sample schedule. Your household routine will dictate what timetable you will set up. Chapter 8, Basic Training, discusses housetraining in more detail.

PREVENTION

Many of the commonly seen problems with dogs can be avoided through simple prevention. Puppy-proofing your house is one means of prevention— making sure plants and cords are out of the way and closet doors are closed.

Puppies go through lots of changes as they grow.

Supervising the dog is another means of prevention. Your German Shepherd can't chew up your sofa if you supervise him while he's in the house with you and if you put him in his crate or outside in his pen when you can't watch him. By supervising the dog, you can teach him what is allowed and what is not. Using the sofa as an example again, if your German Shepherd puppy decides to take a nibble out of the sofa cushion and you are paying attention, you can tell the puppy, "Aack! No!" as he grabs the cushion. Then, you will follow through by handing your puppy one of his chew toys: "Here, chew on this instead." You have prevented potential damage and, at the same time, taught your dog what he should chew.

TIME WITH YOUR DOG

German Shepherds are very people-oriented dogs and must spend time with their owners. Your dog should be inside with you when you are home and next to your bed at night. In addition, you will need to make time to play with your dog, train her and make sure that she gets enough exercise.

With a little thought, it's amazing how creative people can be with their schedules. To spend time with your dog in the morning, getting up thirty minutes earlier will give you time for a fifteen- to twenty-minute walk before taking your shower. If you work close to home, your lunch hour might be just enough time to get home and eat your lunch as you throw the Frisbee for your dog. In the evening, take the children with you as you walk the dog; you can find out what's going on with the kids as you exercise and train your dog.

CRATE TRAINING

Adding a puppy to your household can be a wonderful experience, but it can sour quickly if the puppy is ruining your carpets and chewing up your shoes. There is a training tool that can help—a crate. Two types of crates are commonly used. The first is a heavy plastic molded carrier, much like those the airlines require. The second is made of heavy metal wire bars. The choice of which to use is strictly personal preference, but whatever you choose should be large enough for an adult dog to stand up, turn around and lie down in.

Your puppy will be happiest on a set schedule.

A crate allows you to use the dog's natural denning instinct, the instinct that causes dogs to curl up behind the chair or under a table when they nap. Puppies also have a natural instinct not to soil (relieve themselves in) the place where they sleep. A crate helps housetrain a puppy by using that instinct.

Introduce the crate by opening the door and tossing a treat or toy inside. Allow the puppy to come and go as he pleases, and to investigate the crate. When he is going in and out after the treat or toy, give him a treat and close the door. Leave the door closed for a few minutes and then let the puppy out if, and only if, the puppy is being quiet. If the puppy is throwing a temper tantrum, don't let him out. If you do, you will have taught your puppy that a temper tantrum works to get out.

Put the puppy in her crate when you are home and can't supervise her or when you are busy, such as eating a meal. Put the puppy in the crate when she is over-stimulated—time-outs are good for puppies, too. And, of course, put the puppy in her crate for the night.

Never leave the puppy in the crate longer than four hours, except at night when the crate is next to your bed. It takes a while for the puppy to develop good bowel and bladder control, and you need to be able to let the puppy out when it's time.

Feeding
your
German Shepherd Dog

The Importance of Good Nutrition

GOOD HEALTH

A healthy German Shepherd has bright, alert eyes and a shiny coat, and he conveys the impression of restrained power and energy. Although good health comes from many things, including the dog's genetic heritage and his overall care and environment, good nutrition is vitally important to good health.

Many dogs can carry on for a long time on a substandard diet; in fact, it's amazing how well some dogs do live on scraps, garbage and whatever is tossed their way. But as with all dogs, the German Shepherd's body requires certain substances that she cannot manufacture herself; she must get these from the food she eats. Eventually, poor nutrition shows up as skin problems, dull, dry coat, poor stools, behavior problems, immune system deficiencies, susceptibility to disease and, eventually, a much shorter life span.

WHAT IS NUTRITION?

Nutrition is a constantly ongoing process that starts at conception and ends only with death. Drs. James Sokolowski, DVM, Ph.D. and Manager of the Gaines Nutrition Center, and Anthony Fletcher, DVM and Staff Veterinarian, said, in the Basic Guide to Canine Nutrition (published by Gaines Professional Services, Chicago, Illinois), that "Nutrition may be defined as the process of assimilating food for the biochemical process of living." In other words, anything the dog ingests and digests can give him some kind of nutrition. However, what the dog eats, the food's actual digestibility and how the dog's body uses that food can all affect the actual nutrition gained by eating.

**HOW MANY MEALS
A DAY?**

Individual dogs vary in how much they should eat to maintain a desired body weight—not too fat, but not too thin. Puppies need several meals a day, while older dogs may need only one. Determine how much food keeps your adult dog looking and feeling her best. Then decide how many meals you want to feed with that amount. Like us, most dogs love to eat, and offering two meals a day is more enjoyable for them. If you're worried about overfeeding, make sure you measure correctly and abstain from adding tidbits to the meals.

Whether you feed one or two meals, only leave your dog's food out for the amount of time it takes her to eat it—10 minutes, for example. Freefeeding (when food is available any time) and leisurely meals encourage picky eating. Don't worry if your dog doesn't finish all her dinner in the allotted time. She'll learn she should.

Nutritional Building Blocks

PROTEIN

Proteins are a varied group of biological compounds that affect many different functions in your German Shepherd's body, including the immune system, cell structure and growth. As true omnivores, dogs can digest protein from many different sources. The most common are meats, grains, dairy products and legumes.

Dr. Ben Sheffy, Professor of Nutrition at Cornell University, suggests that puppies should eat a diet consisting of 24 percent digestible protein. Pregnant bitches, working adult dogs or active young adults should eat 20 percent protein, and nonworking adults should eat 16 percent protein.

Carbohydrates

Carbohydrates, like proteins, have many functions in the dog's body, including serving as structural components of cells. However, the most important function is serving as an energy source. Carbohydrates can be found in grains and other plants. The most common sources of carbohydrates include potatoes, rice, noodles and other pastas, and grain and cereal products. Dr. Sheffy recommends a 44 percent carbohydrate diet for nonworking adult dogs; a 38 percent diet for working adults, pregnant bitches and young adults; and 32 percent for puppies.

Always have cool, fresh water available for your dogs.

Fat

Fats have many uses in the body. Fats are the most important form of energy storage, are structural cell elements and are vital to the absorption of several different vitamins. Certain fats are also beneficial to keeping the skin and coat healthy. Fats in dog foods are found primarily in meat and dairy products. Recommended levels are 10 percent for nonworking adult dogs; 12 percent for working dogs, young adults and pregnant bitches; and 14 percent for puppies.

Vitamins

Contrary to popular belief, vitamins do not supply energy but rather are vital elements necessary for growth and the maintenance of life. Vitamins A, E and B are all important to fighting disease and maintaining a strong immune system. There are two classes of vitamins: water soluble and fat soluble. Water-soluble vitamins include the B and B-complex vitamins, C, thiamin, riboflavin, biotin and folic acid. Fat-soluble vitamins include A, D, E and K.

The B vitamins serve a number of different functions, including the metabolism of carbohydrates and amino acids. The B vitamins are very involved in many biochemical processes, and deficiencies can show up as weight loss, slow growth, dry, flaky skin or even anemia, depending upon the specific deficiency. The B vitamins can be obtained from meat and dairy products.

Vitamin C is a controversial vitamin. Some respected sources state that it is not a required dietary vitamin for dogs, yet others regard C as a miracle vitamin for dogs, like it is for people. Some feel it can help prevent hip dysplasia and other potential problems, but these claims have not been proven.

Vitamin C is water soluble, so if you decide to give it to your dog and your dog's body does not metabolize it, it will be discarded in the urine and, therefore, will not hurt the dog. As with any vitamin, ask your veterinarian for his or her recommendation before giving it to your dog.

Vitamin A deficiencies show up as slow or retarded growth, reproductive failure and skin and vision problems. Green and yellow vegetables are the best sources of vitamin A, as are carrots, fish oils and animal livers.

HOW TO READ THE DOG FOOD LABEL

With so many choices on the market, how can you be sure you are feeding the right food for your dog? The information is all there on the label—if you know what you're looking for.

Look for the nutritional claim right up top. Is the food "100% nutritionally complete"? If so, it's for nearly all life stages; "growth and maintenance," on the other hand, is for early development; puppy foods are marked as such, as are foods for senior dogs.

Ingredients are listed in descending order by weight. The first three or four ingredients will tell you the bulk of what the food contains. Look for the highest-quality ingredients, like meats and grains, to be among them.

The Guaranteed Analysis tells you what levels of protein, fat, fiber and moisture are in the food, in that order. While these numbers are meaningful, they won't tell you much about the quality of the food. Nutritional value is in the dry matter, not the moisture content.

In many ways, seeing is believing. If your dog has bright eyes, a shiny coat, a good appetite and a good energy level, chances are his diet's fine. Your dog's breeder and your veterinarian are good sources of advice if you're still confused.

MINERALS

Minerals, like vitamins, are necessary for life and physical well-being. Minerals can affect the body in many ways. A deficiency of calcium can lead to rickets, a deficiency of manganese can cause reproductive failure, and a zinc deficiency can lead to growth retardation and skin problems.

Many minerals are tied in with vitamins; in other words, a vitamin deficiency will also result in a mineral deficiency. For example, an adequate amount of vitamin B_{12} ensures there is also an adequate amount of cobalt because cobalt, a mineral, is a constituent of B_{12}.

WATER

It may seem like common sense to say that your German Shepherd will need water, but the importance of water cannot be emphasized enough. Water makes up about 70 percent of a dog's weight. Water facilitates the generation of energy, the transportation of nutrients and the disposal of wastes. Water is in the bloodstream, in the eyes, in the cerebrospinal fluid and in the gastrointestinal tract. Water is vital to all of the body's functions in some way.

Commercial Dog Foods

BIG BUSINESS

Dog food sales in the United States are a huge business with tremendous competition among manufacturers. This is wonderful for dog owners, as the competition has created a number of feeding alternatives.

The major food companies have research departments that are constantly searching for ways to satisfy the dog owner and the dog. By offering a number of different foods, manufacturers hope to have a product to fit every owner's requirements.

For example, research is continuing to determine the needs of dogs at different life stages. What do puppies need for good growth and development? What do senior dogs need? How about pregnant or lactating bitches? What do dogs with allergies or illnesses require? There are foods for every stage of the dog's life, from puppy through senior citizen, including foods for allergic or ill dogs. All of this continuing research is aimed at providing better nutrition for dogs throughout their lives.

Make sure your puppy has more to chew on than his food.

QUALITY VARIES

A good quality food is necessary for your German Shepherd's health. Because dog food is such a big business, the foods available vary in quality, from the very good to the terrible. To make sure you are using a high-quality food, read the labels on the dog-food packages (see the sidebar, "How to Read the Dog Food Label"). Make sure the food offers the levels of protein, carbohydrates and fats recommended earlier in this chapter.

Read the list of ingredients, too. If one of the first ingredients listed is "by-products," be leery of the food. Dog-food manufacturers can meet protein requirements by including by-products such as hair, feathers, hooves, feet, beaks, diseased tissues and other inferior forms of protein.

German Shepherds do well on a dog food that uses meat and bone meal as the first two or three ingredients. Steer away from foods with a lot of soy or soy products, as these are thought to contribute to stomach gas, which can lead to bloat (for more on this disease, see Chapter 7, Keeping Your German Shepherd Dog Healthy). Some German Shepherds also have allergies to wheat, so you may wish to avoid wheat-based dry foods.

DRY OR CANNED?

Dog foods traditionally come in two different forms: dry and canned. The raw materials for dry foods are mixed together, forced through an extruder (which gives them their shape), then baked or dried. Canned foods are cooked at a high temperature and then sealed in cans.

The water or moisture content of canned food is much higher, as is the meat content. For that reason, most dogs, when given a choice, prefer canned food over dry. Although ounce for ounce the costs may be comparable, the cost of canned food is much higher than that of dry food when you compare the nutrition value of the food. This is because so much of canned food is moisture.

The *Journal of the American Veterinary Medical Association* published research showing that dogs fed a canned diet developed gum disease much earlier in life than did dogs fed a hard kibble diet. The dry food did not eliminate the need for regular dental care, but it helped prevent gum problems.

Very young puppies and older senior dogs may benefit from softer food, perhaps a kibble softened in water or meat juice to make it more palatable and easier to chew. Otherwise, German Shepherds will readily eat and thrive on a high-quality dry dog food.

Dry food is preferred by many dog owners because it has a longer shelf life, is more easily stored, costs less and provides their dogs with tooth and gum exercise. As an added attraction, one German Shepherd owner said, "Dry food also smells better to me. I know my dog loves the smell of canned food, but I don't!"

> ### TO SUPPLEMENT OR NOT TO SUPPLEMENT?
>
> If you're feeding your dog a diet that's correct for her developmental stage and she's alert, healthy-looking and neither over- nor underweight, you don't need to add supplements. These include table scraps as well as vitamins and minerals. In fact, a growing puppy is in danger of developing musculoskeletal disorders by oversupplementation. If you have any concerns about the nutritional quality of the food you're feeding, discuss them with your veterinarian.

COST?

Dog foods are a perfect example of the adage, "You get what you pay for." Many of the cheaper brands of dog foods are made up of lower-cost ingredients, including many by-products. Even though the percentages of proteins and carbohydrates listed on the package look good, that doesn't mean the food is easily or completely digestible. To get the maximum benefit from the food, it must be made of high-quality ingredients and be easily digested.

The end result of a poor diet is an unhealthy dog with large, foul-smelling stools—and higher veterinary bills. It is much better for you and your dog to feed a higher-quality food all the time.

Homemade Diets

WHY?

Dog owners who feed homemade diets usually do so because they are concerned about the quality of commercially available foods. Some owners do not want their dogs eating the additives or preservatives that are in many commercial dog foods. Others cook their dog's food so they can control exactly what their dogs eat.

Breeder Joanne Liebert owns three German Shepherds and cooks her own dog food. "My first German Shepherd had a lot of skin problems," she says, "and when we had him tested, we found that he was allergic to wheat, beef, lamb and soy as well as a number of other things.

TYPES OF FOODS/TREATS

There are three types of commercially available dog food—dry, canned and semimoist—and a huge assortment of treats (lucky dogs!) to feed your dog. Which should you choose?

Dry and canned foods contain similar ingredients. The primary difference between them is their moisture content. The moisture is not just water. It's blood and broth, too, the very things that dogs adore. So while canned food is more palatable, dry food is more economical, convenient and effective in controlling tartar buildup. Most owners feed a 25% canned/75% dry diet to give their dogs the benefit of both. Just be sure your dog is getting the nutrition he needs (you and your veterinarian can determine this).

Semimoist foods have the flavor dogs love and the convenience owners want. However, they tend to contain excessive amounts of artificial colors and preservatives.

Dog treats come in every size, shape and flavor imaginable, from organic cookies shaped like postmen to beefy chew sticks. Dogs seem to love them all, so enjoy the variety. Just be sure not to overindulge your dog. Factor treats into her regular meal sizes.

It's very hard to find a good-quality dog food that doesn't have some or all of these ingredients, so I consulted with a couple of different allergists, dietitians and doctors and made up my own diet." Her allergic dog is now twelve years old and in good health, she reports, and her other two German Shepherds are on the same diet.

One of the biggest problems with a homemade diet is ensuring that it is balanced. Years of research have gone into most commercial diets, and there is no way we can duplicate that work. If you decide you want to cook for your German Shepherd, talk to your veterinarian first. He or she might want to refer you to a nutritional specialist.

Feeding Your Dog

FREEFEED OR SET TIMES?

Many dog owners like to fill a bowl of dog food and leave it out all day, letting the dog munch at will. Although it may be convenient, it is not a good idea for several reasons. First of all, the bowl of food may attract birds, squirrels and ants.

When you are housetraining your puppy, freefeeding makes it difficult to set up a routine. Your puppy will need to relieve himself after eating, and if he munches all day long, you won't be able to tell when he should go outside.

Last, but certainly not least, your dog needs to know that you are the giver of the food, and how better for him to learn it than when you hand him a bowl twice a day? If the food is always available, you are not the one giving it; it's always there—at least as far as your dog is concerned.

HOW MUCH?

Each and every German Shepherd needs a different amount of food. The dog's individual body metabolism, her activity rate and lifestyle all affect her nutritional needs.

Most dog food manufacturers print a chart on the bag showing how much to feed your dog. It's important to note that these are suggested guidelines. If your puppy or dog is soft, round and fat, cut back on the food. If your dog is thin and always hungry, give her more food.

MEALTIMES

Feed your German Shepherd after you have eaten. Again, this may not seem important to you, but to a dog, the most dominant dog always eats first. Since your German Shepherd must see you as the boss, the equivalent of the dominant dog, you need to eat first.

Most experts recommend that puppies eat two to three times a day and adult dogs eat once or twice a day. Most dogs do very well with two meals, 10 or 12 hours apart, so feed your dog after you eat breakfast and then again after you have dinner.

While you are eating, don't feed your German Shepherd from the table or toss him scraps. Not only will this weaken your position as the dominant family member, but it will cause him to beg from anyone at the table—a very bad habit.

SNACKS

An occasional dog biscuit or training treat will not spoil your German Shepherd's appetite, but don't get in the habit of offering treats. Very many American dogs are overweight, and obesity is a leading killer of dogs. When you do offer treats, offer either treats made specifically for dogs or something low in calories and nutritious, like a carrot. Don't offer candy, cookies, left-over tacos or anything like that. Your German Shepherd doesn't need sugar, chocolate is deadly for dogs and spicy foods can cause diarrhea and an upset stomach. Play it safe and give your German Shepherd good quality, nutritious snacks very sparingly.

chapter 6

Grooming
your
German Shepherd Dog

Coat Care

TYPE OF COAT

The German Shepherd's wonderful double coat helps make it a versatile working dog, able to function in just about any climate. This double coat, with coarse outer guard hair and thick, softer undercoat, is also easy to keep up. It does not matt (tangle into knots), nor does it need to be trimmed.

This coat does have a drawback, though: It sheds! German Shepherds shed heavily twice a year, normally in the spring and fall, although the exact time depends upon your climate and the dog's living conditions. However, the coat sheds a little all the time, all year round.

BRUSHING

If you brush your German Shepherd thoroughly two to three times a week, you can keep the hair on the floor and carpet to a minimum. There are three grooming tools you should use when brushing your German Shepherd.

A *pin brush* looks like a woman's hairbrush. It usually has an oval head with numerous metal, pin-like bristles. This brush will go through the coat down to the skin and will loosen clumps of coat, dirt, grass seeds, burrs or other debris. Use this brush first.

To brush your dog, lie him on his side and sit or kneel next to him so that you and he both can relax. Then, starting at his head, begin brushing in the direction the coat grows. Brush with the coat, from the head down to the tip of the tail. Then roll your dog over and do the same thing on the other side.

Your dog will come to love her grooming sessions.

The next tool you will use is a *shedding blade.* This looks like a flexible saw blade bent into a U shape with a handle holding both blades together. This does not go through the coat but, instead, will pull out all the dead coat. With your dog still lying on his side, repeat your previous pattern, going over the dog from head to tail on each side.

You will finish by going over the dog completely with a *slicker brush.* This will gather all the loose coat the other brushes left behind. Follow the same pattern. You may wish to introduce your dog to the *canister vacuum.* If he will tolerate it, this will help tremendously to get the last shedding coat off the dog. When you're done brushing your German Shepherd, you should have a dog with a clean shiny coat and a garbage bag (or vacuum bag) full of loose hair.

Depending upon your German Shepherd's living environment, you may wish to bathe her once a week or once a month. If your dog is a working therapy dog, visiting nursing homes and hospitals, she will need to be bathed prior to each visit. If your dog helps herd sheep and then stays inside at night, she'll need to be bathed often. On the other hand, if your dog lives in the house with you and rarely plays outside, she may stay clean and odor free for weeks at a time. It doesn't matter how often you bathe your dog—even weekly won't hurt her—as long as you use a shampoo formulated for dogs that is gentle and conditioning.

When choosing a shampoo, ask your veterinarian or a dog groomer for recommendations; there are many shampoos on the market. When you buy the shampoo, read the label carefully. Some shampoos are to be diluted in water, a capful or half a cup to a gallon of water. Other shampoos are formulated to use as is. Other shampoos, especially those formulated to kill fleas or ticks, must remain on the dog for two to five minutes before being rinsed off. To make sure you use the shampoo correctly, read the entire label.

A well-groomed dog is a pleasure to look at.

You can bathe your dog outside if the weather is warm and the water from your hose isn't too cold, or you can bathe him in the bathtub. Either way, change into old clothes (you will get wet!) and leash your dog. Put a cotton ball in each of his ears so you don't get water in them. Make sure he is thoroughly brushed first, then use the hose or shower to get him entirely wet. It can be hard sometimes to wet the dog clear to the skin; that wonderful double coat repels water well.

Once your German Shepherd is wet, put some shampoo on your hands and start working into the coat, starting at the head and ears and working down the neck. Be careful not to get soap in her eyes. Continue until the dog is covered with shampoo; don't forget her legs, tummy, groin and tail. Start rinsing in the same way, starting at her head and working down the body. Rinse thoroughly; any soap left on her body could cause her to scratch, even cause a rash.

If you live in an area where fleas and ticks are prevalent and you need to dip your dog, make sure you read and follow the directions carefully. Dips are insecticides and, as such, are poisonous. Used improperly, they can cause you or your dog great harm. So be careful.

Once your German Shepherd is thoroughly rinsed, let him shake off the excess water; then, before you towel him off, go get your canister vacuum. Put the hose on the air exit port so the vacuum is blowing air instead of sucking air, and use that air stream to blow the excess water off your dog. Now towel dry him and, if you wish, use your blow-dryer to finish drying him. Just remember blow-dryers can get very hot, so be careful not to burn him with it.

Other Details

EARS

Each time you brush your German Shepherd, you should check her ears for dirt, wax buildup and foreign objects such as foxtails, burrs or grass seeds. Obviously, any foreign objects should be removed; if you see something you can't get, call your veterinarian immediately. If the dog's ears have a sour smell or seem to be extremely dirty, or if the dog is pawing at her ears or shaking her head, call your veterinarian immediately.

If the dog's ears are dirty or waxy, dampen a cotton ball with witch hazel and, using your finger, gently swab out the ear, getting the cotton ball into all the cracks and crevasses of the ear. You may want to use two or three cotton balls per ear.

GROOMING TOOLS

pin brush

slicker brush

flea comb

towel

matt rake

grooming glove

scissors

nail clippers

tooth-cleaning equipment

shampoo

conditioner

clippers

EYES

If your German Shepherd has some matter in the corners of his eyes, just use a damp paper towel to wipe it off; it's just like the sleep matter you sometimes have when you wake up. However, if your dog has a different type of discharge, or his eyes are red and irritated, call your veterinarian.

TEETH

If you start when your German Shepherd is a puppy, keeping her teeth clean can be easy. Take some gauze from your first-aid kit and wrap it around your index finger. Dampen it and dip it in baking soda. Take that baking soda and rub it over your dog's teeth, working gently over each tooth, the inside and the outside, and into the gum line, taking care not to hurt the dog.

The rubbing action of the rough gauze and the chemical characteristics of the baking soda will help prevent plaque formation and will get rid of the bacteria that form on the teeth and gums.

A clean dog is a happy dog.

Do two or three teeth and let your dog have a drink. Then work on a couple more. You may even want to break it into several sessions, doing half or a quarter of the dog's mouth at each session.

Dr. Paul Richieri, a veterinarian from Oceanside, California, recommends daily teeth cleaning. If daily cleaning is not possible or feasible, however, he said that teeth should be cleaned thoroughly at least three times a week.

NAILS

Your dog's toenails need to be trimmed regularly, preferably once a week. If the nails get too long, they can actually deform the foot by applying pressure against the ground, causing the toes to be in an unnatural position. Long nails are more prone to breaking and tearing, too, and that can be as painful to the dog as it is when we tear a long fingernail. However, if the nails are trimmed regularly, you can keep them short and healthy.

There are two basic types of toenail clippers. One is shaped much like a pair of scissors, and the other has a guillotine-type blade. The type you choose is up to you; both work well—it's simply a matter of what is comfortable to you.

With your clippers in hand, have your dog lie down on the floor in front of you. Take one foot and pull the hair back from the nail so you can see the entire nail. If your dog's nails are black, you won't be able to see the quick, but if your German Shepherd has one or two white nails, you will be able to see the pink quick inside. If, when you trim the nails, you cut into the quick, the nail will bleed and your dog will cry. The quick is just like your nailbed and hurts just as much.

Regular nail care is essential!

If your dog has a white nail, you can use it as a guide in determining how much to trim. However, if your dog's nails are all black, you will have to take it a little slower. Look at the nail's shape. It is arch-shaped, and at the end, if the nails are long, there is a slight hook. You can safely trim that hook without hitting the quick. Then, very carefully, take off just a little more.

Obviously, you will know when you hit the quick—you'll feel guilty because your dog is crying and bleeding. Don't panic. Take a bar of soap from the bathroom and rub the nail along the soap. The soap will clog the nail for a few minutes until the nail can clot. Now, while the soap is in the nail, hold that paw and look at the nail you cut. How far did you go? Trim the other nails, using that one as a guide but taking less off the other nails.

Many dogs dislike having their nails trimmed. Some will whine or cry so much you may even think you have cut into the quick. Other dogs will try to escape from you, fighting and wiggling. If your German Shepherd dislikes nail trimming, try to make it as pleasant as possible. Have the nail clippers at hand, but hidden, perhaps in your pocket. Have your dog lie down in front of you, and then give him a massage, slowly and gently. When the dog is relaxed, touch one of his feet, also slowly and gently. Then go back to massaging; then touch his feet again. By doing this, you are showing him that touching his feet is painless and is followed by more massaging.

Shiny coat and eyes are signs of good health.

When your dog will let you touch his paws without reacting, have the nail clippers in hand as you massage, and then trim one nail. Trim just one, and then go back to massaging. When he is relaxed, trim one more. And so on. If your dog is very frightened of nail trimming, you may even want to break this down even further, doing one paw per massage session.

Common Sense

A healthy German Shepherd should have a shiny coat, clean ears and short nails. The dog shouldn't smell or be offensive in any way. Use your common sense when grooming your dog. If you are unfamiliar with a shampoo, dip or other grooming product, read the label. If you feel that a certain product might be too harsh, or might be dangerous to you, don't use it on your dog. If you have questions, call a local groomer.

chapter 7

Keeping your
German Shepherd
Dog
Healthy

Preventive Health Care

DAILY ROUTINE

Your German Shepherd cannot take care of herself. When you brought your dog home, you assumed the responsibility of caring for her—not just making sure the dog is fed and brushed, but also checking her nails, making sure vaccinations are up to date and getting the dog to the veterinarian when necessary. The easiest way to make sure your dog is well cared for is to set up a routine, then each and every day follow this routine without fail.

Once a day, you need to **run your hands over your German Shepherd**, not just over the coat as you would do when you pet your dog, but, instead, running your fingers through and under the coat so you can feel the dog's skin. As you do this, you will get to know the feel of your dog. Should a tick latch on and bury its head in your dog's skin, you will feel it with your fingers. If your dog cuts himself, or has a lump or bruise or a skin rash, you will feel it. By checking the dog like this every day, you will find these things before they turn into bigger problems.

The best time for this exam is after you have brushed your German Shepherd, when you and the dog will both be relaxed. After you finish brushing your dog, put the brushes down and, starting at the dog's head again, run your hands over your dog's head, around the muzzle, over the skull, feeling around the base of the ears, through the thick neck hair, making sure you touch every square inch of skin. Take your time as you do this. Think of it as giving your dog a gentle massage. Your dog may go to sleep as you massage, but make sure you don't. Stay alert and look for potential problems.

As you massage and examine your German Shepherd, become familiar with every part of her body. Let your hands and fingers **learn what your dog feels like**. Run your hands over the shoulders, down the front legs, over the rib cage and down the back to the hips. Run your hands down each leg, handling each toe on each paw, checking for burrs and foxtails, cuts and scratches. Don't forget to run your hands down the tail, too, checking for lumps, bumps and burrs.

In Chapter 6, we discussed how to clean your German Shepherd's teeth during your regular grooming sessions. It is also important to **check the teeth on a regular basis**, looking for inflamed gums, foreign objects or possible cracked or broken teeth. So as you massage your dog's head, open the mouth and take a look. Look at the inside of the teeth and the outside. Become familiar with what the teeth look like so you will spot a problem, should your dog have one some time in the future.

A German Shepherd's ears are one of the hallmarks of the breed. In Chapter 6, we discussed how to clean the inside of the ears, gently wiping them with cotton balls moistened with witch hazel or a commercial product made especially for cleaning the ears. You can do this after brushing your dog, before you do the massage. **As you wipe out the ear, check for scratches or foreign objects** and give the ear a sniff. If there is quite a bit of discharge and the ear has a sour smell, call your veterinarian; your dog may have an ear infection.

Some German Shepherds have skin allergies. The culprit causing the allergic reaction might be a certain ingredient in the shampoo you are using, pollen from the nearby field or even an ingredient in the food the dog is eating. Skin allergies can show up as red skin, a rash, hives or a weeping, oozing sore. If, during your daily exam, you see a skin problem starting, get your German Shepherd in to your veterinarian right away. It's much easier to treat a skin problem when it's first starting than it is later when the problem has spread and the dog is tormented by the itching. Your veterinarian might also be able to help you identify the cause of the reaction.

During your daily exam, check also for cuts, scrapes, bruises and sores. If you find any minor cuts and scrapes, you can wash them off with soap and water and apply a mild antibiotic ointment. However, if a cut is gaping or looks red and inflamed, call your veterinarian.

A side benefit of this daily exam will show up when you need to take your German Shepherd to the

FIGHTING FLEAS

Remember, the fleas you see on your dog are only part of the problem—the smallest part! To rid your dog and home of fleas, you need to treat your dog *and* your home. Here's how:

• Identify where your pet(s) sleep. These are "hot spots."

• Clean your pets' bedding regularly by vacuuming and washing.

• Spray "hot spots" with a non-toxic, long-lasting flea larvicide.

• Treat outdoor "hot spots" with insecticide.

• Kill eggs on pets with a product containing insect growth regulators (IGRs).

• Kill fleas on pets per your veterinarian's recommendation.

veterinarian; your dog will be used to intimate handling and will not be as stressed by it as a dog that is not handled in this manner.

Common Problems

EXTERNAL PARASITES

Fleas A flea is a small insect about the size of the head of a pin. It is crescent shaped, has six legs and is a tremendous jumper. Fleas live by biting the host animal and eating its blood.

You can see fleas by back-brushing the coat and looking at the skin. A flea will appear as a tiny darting speck, trying to hide in the hair. Fleas best show up on the dog's belly, near the genitals. You can also tell by having your dog lie on a solid-colored sheet and brushing vigorously. If you see salt-and-pepper–type residue falling to the sheet, your German Shepherd has fleas. The residue is made up of fecal matter (the "pepper") and eggs (the "salt").

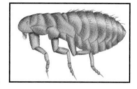

The flea is a die-hard pest.

A heavy infestation can actually kill a dog, especially the very young and very old. Keep in mind that each time a flea bites, it eats a drop or two of blood. Multiply numerous bites a day by the number of fleas, and you can see how dangerous an infestation can be.

Fleas, biting their host, can also cause other problems. Many German Shepherds are allergic to the flea's saliva and scratch each bite until a sore develops. This flea allergy, dermatitis, is a serious problem in many areas of the country. Fleas can also carry disease, such as the infamous bubonic plague, and are the intermediary host for tapeworms, an internal parasite.

To reduce the flea population, you need to treat the dog and its environment. If you treat only the dog and do not treat the house, yard and car, your German Shepherd will simply become reinfected.

There are a number of flea-killing products on the market, including both strong chemical insecticides and natural botanical products. What you decide to use depends upon how bad your flea infestation is and your personal preferences. The stronger chemicals, such as organophosphates and carbamates, will kill the fleas, of course, but they can also kill birds and wildlife. You must read the directions and use them properly.

The natural products are not as strong and some do not kill the flea immediately; sometimes it takes a few hours. Some products use silica or diatomaceous earth to cut or erode the flea's shell so that it dehydrates. There are also commercial products that use natural oils such as pennyroyal, eucalyptus or citrus to repel the fleas. Use these products according to directions, as even natural products can be harmful if used incorrectly.

If you have any questions about what is safe to use on your dog, call your veterinarian or groomer. If you have questions about how to use a particular product, call the manufacturers. They will be more than willing to talk to you and explain exactly how the product should be used. Great survivors, flea eggs can live in the environment for literally years, waiting for the right conditions to hatch; this is not an insect that can be ignored!

Three types of ticks (l-r): the wood tick, brown dog tick and deer tick.

Ticks As you examine your German Shepherd, check also for ticks that may have lodged in the ears or in the hair at the base of the ear, the armpits or around the genitals. If you find a tick, which is a small insect about

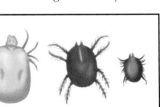

the size of a pencil eraser when engorged with blood, smear it thoroughly with Vaseline. As the tick suffocates in the Vaseline, it will back out and you can then grab it with tweezers and kill it. If the tick doesn't back out, grab it with tweezers and slowly pull it out, twisting very gently. Don't just grab and pull or the tick's head may separate from the body. If the head remains in the skin, an infection or abscess may result and veterinary treatment may be required.

A word of caution: Don't use your fingers or fingernails to pull out ticks. Ticks can carry a number of diseases, including Lyme disease, Rocky Mountain spotted fever and several others, all of which can be very serious. A couple of weeks after removing ticks from her dogs (using her fingers), a friend of mine came down with viral encephalitis, a potentially serious disease. After quizzing her, her doctor felt she got the disease from the ticks. Fortunately, she is now okay, but a pair of tweezers would have saved her and her husband a lot of pain and worry, never mind the medical bills.

Although some flea products are advertised as being able to kill ticks, too, the best way to make sure your German Shepherd is tick free is to examine its body regularly. Make it part of your daily exam.

Use tweezers to remove ticks from your dog.

INTERNAL PARASITES

Roundworms These long, white worms are commonly found internal parasites, especially in puppies, although they occasionally infest adult dogs and people. The adult female roundworm can lay up to 200,000 eggs a day, which are passed out in the dog's feces. Roundworms can be transmitted only via the feces. Because of this, stools should be picked up daily, and your dog should be prevented from investigating other dogs' feces.

If treated early, roundworms are not serious. However, a heavy infestation can severely affect a dog's health. Puppies with roundworms will not thrive and will appear thin, with a dull coat and a pot-bellied appearance. In people, roundworms can be more serious; therefore, early treatment, regular fecal checks and good sanitation are important, both for your German Shepherd's continued good health and yours.

Hookworms Hookworms live their adult lives in the small intestines of dogs. They attach to the intestinal wall and suck blood. When they detach and move to a new location, the old wound continues to bleed because of the anticoagulant the worm injects when it bites. Because of this, bloody diarrhea is usually the first sign of a problem.

Hookworm eggs are passed through the feces. Either they are picked up from the stools, as with roundworms, or, if conditions are right, they hatch in the soil and attach themselves to the feet of their new hosts, where they can burrow into the skin. After burrowing through the skin, they migrate to the intestinal tract, where the cycle starts all over again.

People can pick up hookworms by walking barefoot in infected soil. In the Sunbelt states, children often pick up hookworm eggs when playing outside in the dirt or in a sandbox. Treatment, for both dogs and people, may have to be repeated.

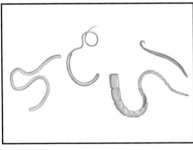

Common internal parasites (l-r): roundworm, whipworm, tapeworm and hookworm.

Tapeworms Tapeworms attach to the intestinal wall to absorb nutrients. They grow by creating new segments, and usually the first sign of an infestation is the ricelike segments found in the stools or on the dog's coat near the rectum. Tapeworms are acquired when a dog chews a flea bite and swallows a flea, the intermediate host. Therefore, a good flea-control program is the best way to prevent a tapeworm infestation.

Whipworms Adult whipworms live in the large intestine, where they feed on blood. The eggs are passed in the stool and can live in the soil for many years. If your dog eats the fresh spring grass, or buries her bone in the yard, she can pick up eggs from the infected soil. If you garden, you can pick up eggs under your fingernails, infecting yourself if you touch your face.

Heavy infestations cause diarrhea, often watery or bloody. The dog may appear thin and anemic, with poor coat. Severe bowel problems may result. Unfortunately, whipworms can be difficult to detect, as the worms do not continually shed eggs. Therefore, a stool sample may be clear one day and the next day show eggs.

Giardia Giardia is common in wild animals in many areas, so if you take your German Shepherd hiking, camping or herding, it can pick up giardia, just as you can. Diarrhea is one of the first symptoms. If your dog has diarrhea and you and your dog have been out camping, make sure you tell your veterinarian.

Heartworms Adult heartworms live in the upper heart and greater pulmonary arteries, where they damage the vessel walls. Poor circulation results, which in turn causes damage to other bodily functions; eventually death from heart failure results.

The adult worms produce thousands of tiny larvae called microfilaria. These circulate throughout the bloodstream until they are sucked up by an intermediate host, a mosquito. The microfilaria go through the larval stages in the mosquito, then are transferred back to another dog when the mosquito bites again.

Dogs infected with heartworms can be treated if caught early. Unfortunately, the treatment itself can be risky and has killed some dogs. However, preventive medications are available that kill the larvae.

A FIRST-AID KIT

Keep a canine first-aid kit on hand for general care and emergencies. Check it periodically to make sure liquids haven't spilled or dried up, and replace medications and materials after they're used. Your kit should include:

Activated charcoal tablets

Adhesive tape
(1 and 2 inches wide)

Antibacterial ointment
(for skin and eyes)

Aspirin (buffered or enteric coated, *not* Ibuprofen)

Bandages: Gauze rolls (1 and 2 inches wide) and dressing pads

Cotton balls

Diarrhea medicine

Dosing syringe

Hydrogen peroxide (3%)

Petroleum jelly

Rectal thermometer

Rubber gloves

Rubbing alcohol

Scissors

Tourniquet

Towel

Tweezers

Heartworm can be diagnosed by a blood test, and a negative result is required before starting the preventive.

INFECTIOUS DISEASES

The diseases listed below can all be prevented, to a certain extent, by vaccinating your German Shepherd, starting when he is a puppy. Unfortunately, vaccinations are no guarantee that he will not get sick. Many factors govern how well a dog reacts to a vaccination, including the antibodies the dog got from his mother, how the dog's own immune system reacts to the vaccine and his general state of health. If you have any questions about vaccinations, call your veterinarian. He or she can answer your questions and recommend a vaccination schedule for your dog.

> ### YOUR PUPPY'S VACCINES
>
> Vaccines are given to prevent your dog from getting an infectious disease like canine distemper or rabies. Vaccines are the ultimate preventive medicine: they're given before your dog ever gets the disease so as to protect him from the disease. That's why it is necessary for your dog to be vaccinated routinely. Puppy vaccines start at eight weeks of age for the five-in-one DHLPP vaccine and are given every three to four weeks until the puppy is sixteen months old. Your veterinarian will put your puppy on a proper schedule and will remind you when to bring in your dog for shots.

Distemper Distemper is a very contagious viral disease that used to kill thousands of dogs. With the effective vaccines available today, it should not kill any dogs but, unfortunately, it still does.

Dogs with distemper are weak and depressed, have a fever and have a discharge from the eyes and nose. Infected dogs cough, vomit and have diarrhea. Intravenous fluids and antibiotics may help support an infected dog but, unfortunately, most die.

A distemper vaccination can normally prevent distemper; however, vaccinations work by stimulating the immune system. If there is a problem with the immune system or if your German Shepherd has not received a complete series of vaccinations, it may not be adequately protected.

Hepatitis Infectious Canine Hepatitis is a highly contagious virus that primarily attacks the liver but can also cause severe kidney damage. It is not related to the form of hepatitis that affects people. The virus is spread through contaminated saliva, mucus, urine or feces. Initial symptoms include depression, vomiting, abdominal pain, high fever and jaundice. Mild cases may be treated with intravenous fluids, antibiotics and even blood transfusions; however, the mortality rate is very high. Vaccinations, usually given in conjunction with the distemper vaccine, can prevent hepatitis.

Coronavirus As is implied by the name, this is also a virus. Coronavirus is rarely fatal to adult dogs, although it is frequently fatal to puppies. The symptoms include vomiting, loss of appetite and a yellowish, watery stool that might contain mucus or blood. The stools carry the shed virus, which is highly contagious.

Fluid or electrolyte therapy can alleviate the dehydration associated with diarrhea, but there is no treatment for the virus itself. There is a vaccine available, which is usually given in combination with the distemper, hepatitis, leptospirosis and parvo vaccinations.

Make sure your puppy gets her shots to keep her healthy.

Parvovirus Parvovirus, or parvo as it is commonly known, is a terrible killer of puppies. A severe gastrointestinal virus, parvo attacks the inner lining of the intestines, causing bloody diarrhea with a distinct odor. In puppies under ten weeks of age, the virus also attacks the heart, causing death, often with no other symptoms. Parvo is so extremely contagious that it has swept through kennels and humane societies, causing multiple deaths in as little as 48 hours.

The gastroenteritis can be treated with fluid therapy and antibiotics; however, the virus moves rapidly, and dehydration can lead to shock and death in a matter of hours. There is a vaccination for parvo, which is often given combined with the distemper, hepatitis, leptospirosis and corona vaccines.

Leptospirosis Leptospirosis is a bacterial disease, rather than a virus. It is spread by infected wildlife, the bacteria being shed in the urine. When your German Shepherd sniffs at a bush that has been urinated on, or drinks from a contaminated stream, he may pick up the bacteria, which then attacks the kidneys, causing kidney failure. Unfortunately, people can also pick up lepto.

Symptoms of lepto include fever, loss of appetite, possible diarrhea and jaundice. Antibiotics can be used to treat the disease, but the outcome is usually not good, due to the serious kidney and liver damage caused by the bacteria. The highly contagious nature of the disease must also be taken into consideration. Other dogs, animals and people are susceptible. Dogs can receive a vaccination for lepto, combined with the distemper, hepatitis, parvo and corona.

Tracheobronchitis Commonly called "canine cough" or "kennel cough," this respiratory infection can be caused by any number of different viral or bacterial agents. These highly contagious, airborne agents can cause a variety of symptoms, including inflammation of the trachea, bronchi and lungs, as well as mild to severe coughing. Antibiotics may be prescribed to combat or prevent pneumonia, and a cough suppressant may quiet the cough.

Some forms of the disease may be prevented by vaccination, but there are so many causes that vaccinations alone cannot prevent tracheobronchitis. Fortunately, the disease is usually mild, and many dogs recover quickly without any treatment at all.

Rabies Rabies is a highly infectious virus usually carried by wildlife, especially bats, raccoons and skunks, although any warm-blooded animals, including humans, may become infected. The virus is transmitted through the saliva, through a bite or break in the skin. The virus then travels up to the brain and spinal cord and throughout the body.

Behavior changes are the first sign of the disease. Nocturnal animals will come out during the day, fearful or shy animals will become bold and aggressive or friendly and affectionate. As the virus spreads, the animal will have trouble swallowing and will drool or salivate excessively. Paralysis and convulsions follow. There is no treatment; however, vaccinations are very effective and are available for people as well as dogs.

Knowing what problems can afflict your German Shepherd Dog can help you notice and treat them sooner.

Problems Particular to the German Shepherd Dog

Autoimmune Problems The dog's immune system protects him from disease; when a virus or bacteria enters the body, white blood cells are triggered to combat the virus or bacteria. In a dog with an immune system problem, the body will not produce these white blood cells; a dog with an autoimmune problem will begin producing white blood cells to attack himself. Although the causes of autoimmune disease can vary, some researchers feel that there is a genetic predisposition toward it. Dogs with any autoimmune disease should not be used for breeding.

Bloat Bloat is the acute dilation of the stomach, caused when the stomach fills with gas and air and, as a result, swells. This swelling prevents the dog from vomiting or passing gas; consequently, the pressure builds, cutting off blood from the heart and to other parts of the body. This causes shock or heart failure, either of which can cause death. Bloat can also cause torsion, where the stomach turns on its long axis, again causing death.

The first symptoms of bloat are obvious. The dog will be pacing or panting, showing signs of distress. The dog's sides will begin to distend. To be successful, treatment should begin at once—there is no time to fool around. If the pressure is not immediately relieved, death can follow within an hour.

To prevent bloat, do not allow your German Shepherd to drink large quantities of water after exercising or after eating. Feed two smaller meals each day instead of one large meal, and limit exercise after eating until a couple of hours have passed. Feed a good-quality food, preferably one that does not expand significantly when wet and does not produce large quantities of gas.

To see how much your dog's food expands, or to see how much gas the food produces, take a handful of the kibble and drop it in a bowl of warm water. Let it set. After 15 minutes, look at the food. Some foods will be wet but will not enlarge. This is good. Other foods will triple their size when wet; this can be dangerous if it happens in your dog's stomach. Some foods will be producing gas bubbles, almost as if they were carbonated. Again, this can be bad news in your dog's stomach.

Cancer Unfortunately, some German Shepherd lineages seem to be prone to cancer. Cancer in dogs, just as in people, is not one disease but a variety of diseases. Although research is continuing, it is unknown how

---

WHEN TO CALL THE VET

In any emergency situation, you should call your veterinarian immediately. You can make the difference in your dog's life by staying as calm as possible when you call and by giving the doctor or the assistant as much information as possible before you leave for the clinic. That way, the vet will be able to take immediate, specific action to remedy your dog's situation.

Emergencies include acute abdominal pain, suspected poisoning, snakebite, burns, frostbite, shock, dehydration, abnormal vomiting or bleeding, and deep wounds. You are the best judge of your dog's health, as you live with and observe him every day. Don't hesitate to call your veterinarian if you suspect trouble.

or why some cells go on a rampage and become cancerous.

When you examine your German Shepherd each day, be aware of any lumps or bumps you might feel, especially as your dog is growing older. Your veterinarian can biopsy any suspicious lump and if it is cancer, many times it can be removed. Early removal has the best chance of success. Unfortunately, cancer is often fatal.

Hip Dysplasia Hip Dysplasia (HD) is a disease of the coxofemoral joint; to put it simply, it is a failure of the head of the femur (thighbone) to fit into the acetabulum (hip socket). HD is not just caused by poorly formed or positioned bones; many researchers feel that the muscles and tendons in the leg and hip may also play a part in the disease.

HD is considered to be a polygenic inherited disorder, which means that many factors come into play. Many different genes may lead to the disease, not just one. Also, environmental factors may lead to HD, including nutrition and exercise, although the part that environmental factors play in the disease is highly debated among experts.

HD can cause a wide range of problems, from mild lameness to movement irregularities to crippling pain. Dogs with HD must often limit their activities, may need corrective surgery or may even need to be put to sleep because of the pain.

Contrary to popular belief, HD cannot be diagnosed by watching a dog run or by the way he lies down; HD can be diagnosed accurately only by X-ray. Once the X-ray is taken, it can be sent to the Orthopedic Foundation for Animals (OFA), which reads, grades and certifies the X-rays of dogs over the age of two years. Sound hips are rated excellent, good or fair, and the dog's owner receives a certificate with the rating. A dysplastic dog will be rated as mild, moderate or severe. Any dog that is found to be dysplastic should be removed from any breeding program and spayed or neutered.

Panosteitis This disease causes lameness and pain in young, rapidly growing puppies, usually between the ages of 6 and 14 months, although it is occasionally seen up to 18 months of age. The lameness usually affects one leg at a time and can sporadically move from one leg to another. Some veterinarians prescribe aspirin to relieve the pain, and most suggest the dog be kept quiet.

Permeal Degeneration This disease is a progressive degeneration of the muscles, connective tissue and skin around the anus. It is not usually associated with infections or impaction of the anal glands, which are located in the same area. Surgery can sometimes remove the problem when done during early stages of the disease; however, the result is often a loose or weak sphincter muscle that allows stools to drop at will—a messy problem.

Thyroid Disease The thyroid gland produces hormones that govern or affect a number of different bodily functions. A dog with a thyroid that is producing less hormones than it should may show symptoms ranging from infertility to dry, dull coat, flaky skin, runny eyes or even difficulty walking. Thyroid problems can be diagnosed with a blood test, and medication can usually relieve the symptoms fairly rapidly. In most cases, the dog will have to remain on the medication for life.

Spaying and Neutering

THE OVERPOPULATION PROBLEM

We have, unfortunately, a tremendous pet overpopulation problem in the United States today. Thousands upon thousands of dogs are destroyed—killed—each year in shelters all over the country. Many of these dogs are purebreds—wonderful dogs who should have had the chance to live out their lives.

The problem has many causes, and it's useless to try to lay blame. However, we can prevent the problem from getting any worse in the future and, we hope, lessen the numbers of dogs being destroyed by spaying and neutering our dogs. By keeping dogs from reproducing, fewer puppies are available for the limited number of homes available.

Spaying and neutering serves other purposes, as well. A male dog that has been neutered (castrated) is less likely to roam, is less likely to show aggression toward other dogs and will be less likely to urinate to mark territory. A female dog in season (receptive to males) will attract hordes of male dogs that wish to breed her. A spayed female dog will, of course, not go through that heat season.

The health benefits of spaying and neutering are numerous. Researchers have found that spayed and neutered dogs have less incidence of cancer later in life—up to 90 percent less. That alone is incredible. In addition, the lessened hormone drive in both males and females makes them much better companions.

BREEDING FOR THE WRONG REASONS

Many people breed, or want to breed, their dogs for the wrong reasons. One of the most common is that they love their pet and want to have a puppy to carry on. Unfortunately, a puppy from their treasured pet will not be the same. The genetic combination that created their pet was from that pet's ancestors. A puppy will be from that pet *and* from the dog to whom they breed the pet. The puppy will be an individual unto itself.

ADVANTAGES OF SPAY/NEUTER

The greatest advantage of spaying (for females) or neutering (for males) your dog is that you are guaranteed your dog will not produce puppies. There are too many puppies already available for too few homes. There are other advantages as well.

ADVANTAGES OF SPAYING

No messy heats.

No "suitors" howling at your windows or waiting in your yard.

Decreased incidences of pyometra (disease of the uterus) and breast cancer.

ADVANTAGES OF NEUTERING

Lessens male aggressive and territorial behaviors, but doesn't affect the dog's personality. Behaviors are often owner-induced, so neutering is not the only answer, but it is a good start.

Prevents the need to roam in search of bitches in season.

Decreased incidences of urogenital diseases.

*A German
Shepherd Dog
has to be in top
form to compete
in dog shows.*

If the owners of a treasured dog want a dog very much like the one they have, they need to go back to the breeder where they got their dog and get another one from the same lineage. That dog, too, will be an individual, but he will be more like their treasured companion.

Another common line of reasoning is that people want their children to see the miracle of birth. The reality, however, is that female dogs want privacy when they give birth, not an audience. Combined with the fact that most puppies are born in the very early morning hours, the kids probably wouldn't see the miracle anyway.

ONLY THE BEST

Many people feel their dog should be allowed to reproduce because she is a purebred or because she has "papers." The fact that a dog is a registered purebred is no assurance of quality, and with the overpopulation problem we are having, only the best dogs should reproduce.

The definition of "best dog" is the dog that best compares with the breed standard; that is healthy, sound, of good personality and temperament; that shows intelligence and trainability; and that has a strong desire to please.

Emergency First Aid

7

ASSESS THE PROBLEM

Keeping Your
German
Shepherd Dog
Healthy

When you are trying to decide what is wrong with your German Shepherd, you will need to play detective. Your dog cannot tell you, "I have a pain right here and I feel like I'm going to throw up." You need to be observant and put the jigsaw pieces together. If you call your veterinarian, he or she will also ask you some questions, and you need to be able to answer those.

What caused you to think there was a problem? What was your first clue there was something wrong? Is your dog eating normally? What do its stools look like? Is the dog limping? When you do a hands-on exam, is the dog sore anywhere? Does it have a lump? Is anything red or swollen? Write down all of these clues and be prepared to tell your veterinarian.

Your vet will also ask you if your dog has a fever. You can take your dog's temperature using a rectal thermometer. Shake the thermometer down and then put some petroleum jelly on it. Using the dog's tail as a guide, insert the thermometer into the anus about an inch. Keep holding the thermometer, don't let go of it, and watch your clock. After three minutes, withdraw the thermometer, wipe it off and read the temperature. Normal is 101 to 102 degrees.

IDENTIFYING YOUR DOG

It's a terrible thing to think about, but your dog could somehow, someday, get lost or stolen. How would you get him back? Your best bet would be to have some form of identification on your dog. You can choose from a collar and tags, a tattoo, a microchip or a combination of these three.

Every dog should wear a buckle collar with identification tags. They are the quickest and easiest way for a stranger to identify your dog. It's best to inscribe the tags with your name and phone number; you don't need to include your dog's name.

There are two ways to permanently identify your dog. The first is a tattoo, placed on the inside of your dog's thigh. The tattoo should be your social security number or your dog's AKC registration number.

The second is a microchip, a rice-sized pellet that's inserted under the dog's skin at the base of the neck, between the shoulder blades. When a scanner is passed over the dog, it will beep, notifying the person that the dog has a chip. The scanner will then show a code, identifying the dog. Microchips are becoming more and more popular and are certainly the wave of the future.

83

The veterinarian will also ask if your dog is vomiting and, if so, what did the vomit look like? Was there anything unusual in it? Did the dog vomit up garbage? A plastic bag? Grass? How often did the dog vomit, just once or is it ongoing?

Similar questions will be asked about the dog's bowel movements. Did the dog have a bowel movement? If so, did it look normal? Was there mucus or blood in the stool? Did the stool have a different or peculiar smell? Did you see any foreign objects in the stool?

Be prepared to answer all these questions, and if you are nervous or scared, write them down.

It is often difficult for dog owners to decide when to call the veterinarian and when they can handle a problem at home. Listed below are some commonly seen problems and some basic advice as to how you might handle them. However, the cost of a telephone call is small compared to your dog's life. When in doubt—call!

Use a scarf or old hose to make a temporary muzzle, as shown.

ANIMAL BITES

Muzzle your dog if he is in pain. Using a pair of panty hose or a long piece of gauze, wrap it around the dog's muzzle, crossing under the jaw, then pulling it around his head, tying it in the back.

Trim the hair from around the wound and liberally pour hydrogen peroxide over it. A hand-held pressure bandage can help stop the bleeding. Stitches may be necessary if the bite is a rip or tear, so call your vet; he or she may also recommend putting the dog on antibiotics.

BEE STINGS

Many dogs are allergic to bee stings and will immediately start to swell. Call your vet immediately. He or she may recommend you give the dog an antihistamine such as Benadryl and instruct you on the dosage.

BLEEDING

Muzzle your dog if she is in pain. Place a gauze pad or, if that is not available, a clean cloth over the wound and apply pressure. If the wound will require stitches or if the bleeding doesn't stop, call your vet. If the wound is on a leg and continues to bleed, apply a tourniquet but make sure it is loosened every 15 minutes. If you use a tourniquet or the wound continues bleeding, get to your vet as soon as possible.

CHOKING

Applying abdominal thrusts can save a choking dog.

If your German Shepherd is pawing at his mouth, gagging, coughing or drooling, he may have something caught in his mouth or throat. Open his jaws and shine a flashlight down the throat. If you can see the object, reach in and pull it out, using your fingers, tweezers or a pair of pliers. If you cannot see anything and your dog is still choking, hit him behind the neck between the shoul-

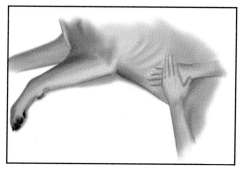

ders to try and dislodge the object. If this fails, use an adapted Heimlich maneuver. Grasp either side of the dog's rib cage and squeeze. Don't break ribs, but try to make a sharp enough movement to cause the air in the lungs to force the object out.

If your dog can breathe around the object, get to the vet as soon as possible. If your dog cannot breathe around the object, you don't have time to move the dog. Keep working on getting the object out.

FRACTURES

Because your German Shepherd will be in great
pain if she has broken a bone, you should muzzle her
immediately. Do not try to set the fracture, but try to
immobilize the limb, if possible, by using a piece of
wood and then wrapping it with gauze or soft cloth. If
there is a door or board you can use as a backboard or
stretcher so the injured limb is stable, use it. Transport
the dog to the vet as soon as possible.

*Make a tempo-
rary splint by
wrapping the
leg in firm
casing, then
bandaging it.*

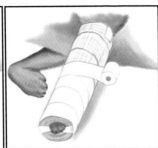

BROKEN NAILS

A ripped or broken toenail can be very painful. If the
dog is frantic, muzzle him to protect yourself. If a piece
of the nail is hanging, trim it off. Run hydrogen peroxide over the nail. If the nail is bleeding, run it over a
soft bar of soap. The soap will help the nail clot. If the
quick is showing or if the nail has broken off under
the skin, call your veterinarian. Antibiotics might be
needed to prevent an infection.

OVERHEATING OR HEATSTROKE

Overheating or heatstroke are characterized by rapid
or difficult breathing, vomiting, even collapse. If your
dog has these symptoms you need to act at once—
this can be life-threatening. Immediately place your
German Shepherd in a tub of cool water or, if a tub is
not available, run water from a hose over your dog. Use
a rectal thermometer to take the dog's temperature
and call your veterinarian immediately. Encourage
your dog to drink some cool water. Transport the dog

to the vet as soon as you can, or as soon as the vet recommends it.

POISONING

Symptoms of poisoning include retching and vomiting, diarrhea, salivation, labored breathing, dilated
pupils, weakness, collapse or convul-
sions. Sometimes one or more symptoms will appear, depending upon
the poison. If you suspect your dog
has been in contact with a poison,
time is critical. Call your veterinarian
right away. If your vet is not immediately available, call the National
Animal Poison Control Center hotline (1-800-548-2423). The hotline

and your vet can better treat your dog if you can tell
them what was ingested and approximately how much.
*Important! Do not make your dog vomit unless instructed to
do so.*

*Some of the
many house-
hold substances
harmful to your
dog.*

SNAKEBITE

Without getting bitten yourself, try to get a look at the
snake, making note of colors, patterns and markings so
you or your vet can identify the snake. Keep the dog as
quiet as possible to restrict the flow of venom. If the
bite is on a leg, apply a tourniquet above the wound.
Loosen the tourniquet every 15 minutes. *Important! Do
not cut X's above the wound.* That often causes more tissue damage than the bite itself, and is not known to be
effective.

If your dog is in pain or is frantic, muzzle him. Call
your vet immediately so that he or she can get some
antivenom medication ready for your dog's arrival.

Home Health Care

GIVING MEDICATION

At some time during your German Shepherd's life, you
will need to give her medication of some kind. Some

medications are easy to give, others are difficult. Along the same lines, some dogs are easy to medicate, others can be very difficult.

To put eye ointment in the eye without poking the dog with the tube, stand behind your dog and cuddle his head up against your legs. With one hand, gently pull the lower eyelid away from the eye just slightly. At the same time, squeeze some of the ointment into the lower eyelid. When the dog closes his eye, the medication will be distributed over the eye.

Squeeze eye ointment into the lower lid.

There are a couple of different ways to give your dog a pill. The easiest way is to hide the pill in a piece of cheese or hot dog. Most dogs will just gulp it down. However, some dogs are very clever and will eat the hot dog and spit out the pill. For those dogs, have the dog sit and then stand behind him, straddling his back. Pull the dog's head up and back so the dog's muzzle is pointing up. Open his mouth and very quickly drop the pill in the back of the throat. Close the dog's mouth and massage his throat until you see the dog swallow. Then, before you let the dog go, open his mouth again and look to make sure he has swallowed the pill.

To give a pill, open the mouth wide, then drop it in the back of the throat.

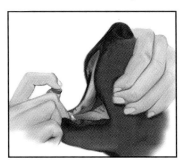

Liquid medication can be given in much the same way, pouring it in the dog's mouth; however, you must take care that the dog doesn't inhale the medication instead of swallowing it. An easier way for many people to give liquids is to measure the amount of medication needed into a baster, such as a chicken or turkey baster, or a large eyedropper. Have the dog sit and then put the tip of the baster into the dog's mouth from the side, between the molars. Holding the dog's mouth shut, squeeze the medication into the dog's mouth while you tilt the dog's head backwards slightly so the medication runs into the mouth instead of out.

Applying skin ointments is usually very easy; you simply rub them into the skin according to directions. Keeping your German Shepherd from licking the ointments off can be more difficult. With some medications or problems it might not make any difference whether or not the dog licks, but in many cases licking will only make the problem worse. A commercially available product called Bitter Apple is very effective for discouraging some dogs; the product tastes bad, and when the dog licks, she is offended by the taste. Bitter Apple is applied around, not on, the wound, as it contains alcohol and stings open wounds. If you need to apply skin medication and your dog is licking, call your veterinarian and ask if you can use Bitter Apple.

If your dog has a bad skin condition that licking will make worse, or if your dog has stitches, your veterinarian might recommend that you put an Elizabethan collar on your dog. Named for the fashion styles of the reign of Queen Elizabeth I, this is a large plastic collar that extends at least to the tip of your dog's nose. It looks like your dog is wearing a huge bucket on its head. The collar is ugly and clumsy, and most dogs absolutely hate it; however, it can prevent your dog from reaching stitches or wounds, giving them time to heal.

An Elizabethan collar keeps your dog from licking a fresh wound.

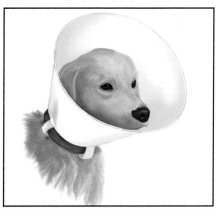

There are two very important things to emphasize about medicating and treating your German Shepherd. First of all, if your veterinarian prescribes a treatment, don't be afraid to ask questions. Ask what the drug is, what it does and how long your dog should take it. Ask if there are any side effects you should watch for. Make sure you understand what your dog's problem is, what the course of treatment will do and what you should (or should not) expect.

Second, make sure you follow through on the course of treatment. If your veterinarian said to give the medication for 10 days, give it for 10 days. Don't stop at five days just because your dog looks better. Again, if you have any problems or reservations, call your vet.

As Your German Shepherd Grows Older

A PRECIOUS TIME

German Shepherds can, on the average, live twelve to fourteen years. However, to live that long, remaining happy and healthy, your German Shepherd will need your help. Aging in dogs, as in people, brings some changes and problems. You will see your dog's vision dim, his hearing fade and his joints stiffen. Heart and kidney disease are common in older dogs. Reflexes will not be as sharp as they once were, and your dog may be more sensitive to heat and cold. Your dog may also get grouchy, showing less tolerance to younger dogs, to children and to things that may not be part of his normal routine.

Run your hands regularly over your dog to feel for any injuries.

An old dog that has lived his life with you is a special gift. Your old German Shepherd knows your ways, your likes and dislikes and your habits. He almost seems able to read your mind, and his greatest joy is simply to be close to you. Your old German Shepherd may not be able to do the work he did when he was younger but he can still be a wonderful companion.

ARTHRITIS

Arthritis is common in old dogs. The joints get stiff, especially when it's chilly. Your German Shepherd may have trouble jumping or getting up in the morning. Give your old dog something soft to sleep on, and keep your old dog warm. Talk to your veterinarian about treatment; there are pain relievers that can help.

NUTRITION

As your dog's activity level slows down, he will need to consume less calories and, as his body ages, he will need less protein. However, some old dogs have a problem digesting foods, too, and this may show up in poor stools and a dull coat. Several dog food manufacturers offer premium-quality foods for senior dogs; these foods are more easily digested by the old dog. A heaping tablespoon of live-culture yogurt will also aid the digestion.

TEETH

Your German Shepherd may need to have her teeth cleaned professionally, and this is something you should not put off doing. Bacteria that build up on the teeth, called plaque, can infect the gums, get into the bloodstream and cause infections in other parts of the body, including the kidneys and heart.

Check your dog's teeth frequently and brush them regularly.

EXERCISE

Exercise is still important to your older German Shepherd. Your dog needs the stimulation of walking around and seeing and smelling the world. Tailor the exercise to your dog's abilities and needs. If your dog can still chase a tennis ball, great! However, as your dog ages, a slow walk about the neighborhood might be enough.

HOME REMEDIES

If you use herbal or home remedies yourself, you might want to use some for your dog. Many people recommend vitamin C for dogs with arthritis. Rose hips, also a good source of vitamin C, is good for the digestion as well. Chamomile tea is calming and good for an upset stomach. Yucca is a natural anti-inflammatory and is wonderful for aches and pains as well as arthritis. For more information, check out your local library for books on herbal medicine; there are many available.

WHEN IT'S TIME

We have the option, with our dogs, not to let them suffer when they are old, ill and infirm. There will be a time when you will need to decide how you are going to handle putting your dog out of his pain. Some feel the time has come when the dog is no longer enjoying life, when he's incontinent and despondent because he has broken house-training. Only you can make the decision, but spare your companion the humiliation of incontinence, convulsions or the inability to stand up or move around.

You and your dog can enjoy many years together if you keep him healthy.

If your German Shepherd must be helped to her death, your veterinarian can give an injection that is an overdose of anesthetic. Your dog will go to sleep and quietly stop breathing. Be there with your dog. Let your arms hold your old friend and let your dog hear your voice saying how much you love her as she goes to sleep. There will be no fear, and the last thing your dog will remember is your love.

GRIEVING

A well-loved dog is an emotional investment of unparalleled returns. Unfortunately, our dogs' lives are entirely too short and we must learn to cope with the inevitable loss of them. Grief is a natural reaction to the loss of a loved one, whether it is a pet, a spouse, friend or family member. Grief has no set pattern; its intensity and duration are different for each person and for each loss.

Sometimes the best outlet for grief is a good hard cry. For other people, talking about their pet is good therapy. However, don't allow people to say, "But it was only a dog." These people obviously don't understand. Talk to people who own dogs, preferably other people who have lost an old dog and understand your loss.

Ceremonies can be good, too, allowing you to say good-bye to your dog and release some tension. Sprinkling your German Shepherd's ashes under a fragrant rose bush or burying your dog under a favorite apple tree will give you a living monument, a place where you can enjoy nature, where you can recall the wonderful times you shared with your German Shepherd.

Hero of the Year

When Girl was discovered by Dorothy Ellis on her and her husband Ray's property one summer day, she was a young, abandoned dog covered with fleas. But after a week of baths and a flea dip, she was looking like a Shepherd again, and she had a new home. Little did Dorothy suspect that the Shepherd would one day return the gift in spades by saving her husband's life.

Dorothy and Ray Ellis with Girl.

The Ellises live in Martins Ferry, Ohio. Girl loved both the Ellises but was particularly fond of doing outdoor work with Ray. One November day Ray was out cutting a tree. He'd brought one load of wood in and went back to cut more. Not too long after, Girl came back to the house and jumped up on the door, so Dorothy let her in. Girl was prancing and whining like something was wrong. Dorothy called to

Ray and got no answer, so she decided to go see where Ray was.

Girl ran out in front of Dorothy, turning around every few feet to make sure she was following. When she got within 30 feet of Ray, Girl stood at attention. When Dorothy saw Ray, she thought he was resting, but she quickly realized he was badly hurt. He'd been hit in the head and was scratched and bleeding, but it was his foot that was most damaged. The chainsaw had cut right through his work boot and there was blood everywhere. While Girl circled around Ray, who was semi-conscious, Dorothy called the emergency squad.

A special surgeon had to be brought into the hospital to sew Ray's foot back together. But he had his foot, and he had his life. Thanks to Girl's quick thinking. "God must have sent her to us," Dorothy said.

The story made several newspapers and earned Girl Ken-L Ration's 1994 Dog Hero of the Year award.

Girl was the 41st winner of the award, which is now co-sponsored by the American Veterinary Medical Association to honor pets that, in addition to being a best friend, are often lifesavers. Another German Shepherd Dog was awarded an honorable mention. Ten-year-old Ranger cared for a female mixed breed trapped in a coyote snare for over a week, bringing her mouthfuls of snow and bits of food, and finally howling incessantly to get someone's attention. Ranger is owned by Leo Martinez of Espanola, New Mexico. Thirty-five families offered to adopt the stray, whose leg had to be amputated, but who survived thanks to Ranger.

Girl is one of six German Shepherd Dogs who've been awarded the Dog Hero award to date, and Ranger is one of many honorable mentions for the breed.

Your Happy, Healthy Pet

Your Dog's Name _____

Name on Your Dog's Pedigree (if your dog has one) _____

_____

Where Your Dog Came From _____

_____

Your Dog's Birthday _____

Your Dog's Veterinarian

    Name _____

    Address _____

    Phone Number _____

    Emergency Number _____

Your Dog's Health

    Vaccines

        type _____ date given _____

        type _____ date given _____

        type _____ date given _____

        type _____ date given _____

    Heartworm

        date tested _____ type used_____ start date _____

Your Dog's License Number_____

Groomer's Name and Number _____

Dogsitter/Walker's Name and Number_____

Awards Your Dog Has Won

    Award _____ date earned _____

    Award _____ date earned _____

Enjoying

your

Dog

chapter **8**

Basic
Training

by Ian Dunbar, Ph.D., MRCVS

Training is the jewel in the crown—the most important aspect of doggy husbandry. There is no more important variable influencing dog behavior and temperament than the dog's education: A well-trained, well-behaved and good-natured puppydog is always a joy to live with, but an untrained and uncivilized dog can be a perpetual nightmare. Moreover, deny the dog an education and it will not have the opportunity to fulfill its own canine potential; neither will it have the ability to communicate effectively with its human companions.

Luckily, modern psychological training methods are easy, efficient and effective and, above all, considerably dog-friendly and user-friendly. Doggy education is as simple as it is enjoyable. But before

you can have a good time play-training with your new
dog, you have to learn what to do and how to do it.
There is no bigger variable influencing the success of
dog training than the *owner's* experience and expertise. *Before you embark on the dog's education, you must first
educate yourself.*

Basic Training for Owners

Ideally, basic owner training should begin well *before*
you select your dog. Find out all you can about your
chosen breed first, then master rudimentary training
and handling skills. If you already have your
puppy/dog, owner training is a dire emergency—the
clock is running! Especially for puppies, the first few
weeks at home are the most important and influential
days in the dog's life. Indeed, the cause of most adolescent and adult problems may be traced back to the
initial days the pup explores his new home. This is the
time to establish the *status quo*—to teach the
puppy/dog how you would like him to behave and so
prevent otherwise quite predictable problems.

In addition to consulting breeders and breed books
such as this one (which understandably have a positive
breed bias), seek out as many pet owners with your
breed you can find. Good points are obvious. What you
want to find out are the breed-specific *problems*, so you
can nip them in the bud. In particular, you should talk
to owners with *adolescent* dogs and make a list of all
anticipated problems. Most important, *test drive* at least
half a dozen adolescent and adult dogs of your breed
yourself. An eight-week-old puppy is deceptively easy to
handle, but she will acquire adult size, speed and
strength in just four months, so you should learn now
what to prepare for.

Puppy and pet dog training classes offer a convenient
venue to locate pet owners and observe dogs in action.
For a list of suitable trainers in your area, contact the
Association of Pet Dog Trainers (see Chapter 13). You
may also begin your basic owner training by observing
other owners in class. Watch as many classes and test

drive as many dogs as possible. Select an upbeat, dog-friendly, people-friendly, fun-and-games, puppydog pet training class to learn the ropes. Also, watch training videos and read training books (see Chapter 12). You must find out what to do and how to do it *before* you have to do it.

Principles of Training

Most people think training comprises teaching the dog to do things such as sit, speak and roll over, but even a four-week-old pup knows how to do these things already. Instead, the first step in training involves teaching the dog human words for each dog behavior and activity and for each aspect of the dog's environment. That way you, the owner, can more easily participate in the dog's domestic education by directing him to perform specific actions appropriately, that is, at the right time, in the right place, and so on. Training opens communication channels, enabling an educated dog to at least understand the owner's requests.

In addition to teaching a dog *what* we want her to do, it is also necessary to teach her *why* she should do what we ask. Indeed, 95 percent of training revolves around motivating the dog *to want to do* what we want. Dogs often understand what their owners want; they just don't see the point of doing it—especially when the owner's repetitively boring and seemingly senseless instructions are totally at odds with much more pressing and exciting doggy distractions. It is not so much the dog who is being stubborn or dominant; rather, it is the owner who has failed to acknowledge the dog's needs and feelings and to approach training from the dog's point of view.

The Meaning of Instructions

The secret to successful training is learning how to use training lures to predict or prompt specific behaviors—to coax the dog to do what you want *when* you want. Any highly valued object (such as a treat or toy) may be used as a lure, which the dog will follow with his eyes and nose. Moving the lure in specific ways entices the dog to move his nose, head and entire body in specific ways. In fact, by learning the art of manipulating various lures, it is possible to teach the dog to assume virtually any body position and perform any action. Once you have control over the expression of the dog's behaviors and can elicit any body position or behavior at will, you can easily teach the dog to perform on request.

Tell your dog what you want him to do, use a lure to entice him to respond correctly, then profusely praise

Teach your dog words for each activity he needs to know, like down.

and maybe reward him once he performs the desired action. For example, verbally request "Fido, sit!" while you move a squeaky toy upwards and backwards over the dog's muzzle (lure-movement and hand signal), smile knowingly as he looks up (to follow the lure) and sits down (as a result of canine anatomical engineering), then praise him to distraction ("Gooood Fido!"). Squeak the toy, offer a training treat and give your dog and yourself a pat on the back.

Being able to elicit desired responses over and over enables the owner to reward the dog over and over. Consequently, the dog begins to think training is fun. For example, the more the dog is rewarded for sitting, the more she enjoys sitting. Eventually the dog comes to realize that, whereas most sitting is appreciated, sitting immediately upon request usually prompts especially enthusiastic praise and a slew of high-level rewards. The dog begins to sit on cue much of the time, showing that she is starting to grasp the meaning of the owner's verbal request and hand signal.

Why Comply?

Most dogs enjoy initial lure/reward training and are only too happy to comply with their owners' wishes. Unfortunately, repetitive drilling without appreciative feedback tends to diminish the dog's enthusiasm until he eventually fails to see the point of complying anymore. Moreover, as the dog approaches adolescence he becomes more easily distracted as he develops other interests. Lengthy sessions with repetitive exercises tend to bore and demotivate both parties. If it's not fun, the owner doesn't do it and neither does the dog.

Integrate training into your dog's life: The greater number of training sessions each day and the *shorter* they are, the more willingly compliant your dog will become. Make sure to have a short (just a few seconds) training interlude before every enjoyable canine activity. For example, ask your dog to sit to greet people, to sit before you throw his Frisbee, and to sit for his supper. Really, sitting is no different from a canine "please." Also, include numerous short training interludes during every enjoyable canine pastime, for example, when playing with the dog or when he is running in the park. In this fashion, doggy distractions may be effectively converted into rewards for training. Just as all games have rules, fun becomes training . . . and training becomes fun.

Eventually, rewards actually become unnecessary to continue motivating your dog. If trained with consideration and kindness, performing the desired behaviors will become self-rewarding and, in a sense, your dog will motivate himself. Just as it is not necessary to reward a human companion during an enjoyable walk in the park, or following a game of tennis, it is hardly necessary to reward our best friend—the dog—for walking by our side or while playing fetch. Human company during enjoyable activities is reward enough for most dogs.

Even though your dog has become self-motivating, it's still good to praise and pet him a lot and offer rewards once in a while, especially for a good job well done. And if for no other reason, praising and rewarding others is good for the human heart.

To train your dog, you need gentle hands, a loving heart and a good attitude.

Punishment

Without a doubt, lure/reward training is by far the best way to teach: Entice your dog to do what you want and then reward him for doing so. Unfortunately, a human shortcoming is to take the good for granted and to moan and groan at the bad. Specifically, the dog's many good behaviors are ignored while the owner focuses on punishing the dog for making mistakes. In extreme cases, instruction is *limited* to punishing mistakes made by a trainee dog, child, employee or husband, even though it has been proven punishment training is notoriously inefficient and ineffective and is decidedly unfriendly and combative. It teaches the dog that training is a drag, almost as quickly as it teaches the dog to dislike his trainer. Why treat our best friends like our worst enemies?

Punishment training is also much more laborious and time consuming. Whereas it takes only a finite amount of time to teach a dog what to chew, for example, it takes much, much longer to punish the dog for each and every mistake. Remember, *there is only one right way!* So why not teach that right way from the outset?!

To make matters worse, punishment training causes severe lapses in the dog's reliability. Since it is obviously impossible to punish the dog each and every time she misbehaves, the dog quickly learns to distinguish between those times when she must comply (so as to avoid impending punishment) and those times when she need not comply, because punishment is impossible. Such times include when the dog is off leash and only six feet away, when the owner is otherwise engaged (talking to a friend, watching television, taking a shower, tending to the baby or chatting on the telephone), or when the dog is left at home alone.

Instances of misbehavior will be numerous when the owner is away, because even when the dog complied in the owner's looming presence, he did so unwillingly. The dog was forced to act against his will, rather than moulding his will to want to please. Hence, when the owner is absent, not only does the dog know he need not comply, he simply does not want to. Again, the trainee is not a stubborn vindictive beast, but rather the trainer has failed to teach.

Punishment training invariably creates unpredictable Jekyll and Hyde behavior.

Trainer's Tools

Many training books extol the virtues of a vast array of training paraphernalia and electronic and metallic gizmos, most of which are designed for canine restraint, correction and punishment, rather than for actual facilitation of doggy education. In reality, most effective training tools are not found in stores; they come from within ourselves. In addition to a willing dog, all you really need is a functional human brain, gentle hands, a loving heart and a good attitude.

In terms of equipment, all dogs do require a quality buckle collar to sport dog tags and to attach the leash (for safety and to comply with local leash laws). Hollow chewtoys (like Kongs or sterilized longbones) and a dog bed or collapsible crate are a must for housetraining. Three additional tools are required:

1. specific lures (training treats and toys) to predict and prompt specific desired behaviors;

2. rewards (praise, affection, training treats and toys) to reinforce for the dog what a lot of fun it all is; and

3. knowledge—how to convert the dog's favorite activities and games (potential distractions to training) into "life-rewards," which may be employed to facilitate training.

The most powerful of these is *knowledge.* Education is the key! Watch training classes, participate in training classes, watch videos, read books, enjoy playtraining with your dog, and then your dog will say "Please," and your dog will say "Thank you!"

Housetraining

If dogs were left to their own devices, certainly they would chew, dig and bark for entertainment and then no doubt highlight a few areas of their living space with sprinkles of urine, in much the same way we decorate by hanging pictures. Consequently, when we ask a dog to live with us, we must teach him *where* he may dig and perform his toilet duties, *what* he may chew and *when* he may bark. After all, when left at home alone for many hours, we cannot expect the dog to amuse himself by completing crosswords or watching the soaps on TV!

Also, it would be decidedly unfair to keep the house rules a secret from the dog, and then get angry and punish the poor critter for inevitably transgressing rules he did not even know existed. Remember, without adequate education and guidance, the dog will be forced to establish his own rules—doggy rules—that most probably will be at odds with the owner's view of domestic living.

Since most problems develop during the first few days the dog is at home, prospective dog owners must be certain they are quite clear about the principles of housetraining *before* they get a dog. Early misbehaviors quickly become established as the status quo—

becoming firmly entrenched as hard-to-break bad habits, which set the precedent for years to come. Make sure to teach your dog good habits right from the start. Good habits are just as hard to break as bad ones!

Ideally, when a new dog comes home, try to arrange for someone to be present for as much as possible during the first few days (for adult dogs) or weeks for puppies. With only a little forethought, it is surprisingly easy to find a puppy sitter, such as a retired person, who would be willing to eat from your refrigerator and watch your television while keeping an eye on the newcomer to encourage the dog to play with chewtoys and to ensure he goes outside on a regular basis.

POTTY TRAINING

To teach the dog where to relieve himself:

1. never let him make a single mistake;
2. let him know where you want him to go; and
3. handsomely reward him for doing so: "GOOOOOOOD DOG!!!" liver treat, liver treat, liver treat!

PREVENTING MISTAKES

A single mistake is a training disaster, since it heralds many more in future weeks. And each time the dog soils the house, this further reinforces the dog's unfortunate preference for an indoor, carpeted toilet. *Do not let an unhousetrained dog have full run of the house if you are away from home or cannot pay full attention.* Instead, confine the dog to an area where elimination is appropriate, such as an outdoor run or, better still, a small, comfortable indoor kennel with access to an outdoor run. When confined in this manner, most dogs will naturally housetrain themselves.

If that's not possible, confine the dog to an area, such as a utility room, kitchen, basement or garage, where elimination may not be desired in the long run but as an interim measure it is certainly preferable to doing it all around the house. Use newspaper to cover the floor of the dog's day room. The newspaper may be used to soak up the urine and to wrap up and dispose of the feces. Once your dog develops a preferred spot for eliminating, it is only necessary to cover that part of the floor with newspaper. The smaller papered area may then be moved (only a little each day) towards the door to the outside. Thus the dog will develop the tendency to go to the door when he needs to relieve himself.

Never confine an unhousetrained dog to a crate for long periods. Doing so would force the dog to soil the crate and ruin its usefulness as an aid for housetraining (see the following discussion).

The first few weeks at home are the most important and influential in your dog's life.

TEACHING WHERE

In order to teach your dog where you would like her to do her business, you have to be there to direct the proceedings—an obvious, yet often neglected, fact of life. In order to be there to teach the dog *where* to go, you need to know *when* she needs to go. Indeed, the success of housetraining depends on the owner's ability to predict these times. Certainly, a regular feeding schedule will facilitate prediction somewhat, but there is

nothing like "loading the deck" and influencing the timing of the outcome yourself!

Whenever you are at home, make sure the dog is under constant supervision and/or confined to a small area. If already well trained, simply instruct the dog to lie down in his bed or basket. Alternatively, confine the dog to a crate (doggy den) or tie-down (a short, 18-inch lead that can be clipped to an eye hook in the baseboard). Short-term close confinement strongly inhibits urination and defecation, since the dog does not want to soil his sleeping area. Thus, when you release the puppydog each hour, he will definitely need to urinate immediately and defecate every third or fourth hour. Keep the dog confined to his doggy den and take him to his intended toilet area each hour, every hour, and on the hour.

When taking your dog outside, instruct him to sit quietly before opening the door—he will soon learn to sit by the door when he needs to go out!

TEACHING WHY

Being able to predict when the dog needs to go enables the owner to be on the spot to praise and reward the dog. Each hour, hurry the dog to the intended toilet area in the yard, issue the appropriate instruction ("Go pee!" or "Go poop!"), then give the dog three to four minutes to produce. Praise and offer a couple of training treats when successful. The treats are important because many people fail to praise their dogs with feeling . . . and housetraining is hardly the time for understatement. So either loosen up and enthusiastically praise that dog: "Wuzzzer-wuzzer-wuzzer, hoooser good wuffer den? Hoooo went pee for Daddy?" Or say "Good dog!" as best you can and offer the treats for effect.

Following elimination is an ideal time for a spot of playtraining in the yard or house. Also, an empty dog may be allowed greater freedom around the house for the next half hour or so, just as long as you keep an eye out to make sure he does not get into other kinds of mischief. If you are preoccupied and cannot pay full attention, confine the dog to his doggy den once more to enjoy a peaceful snooze or to play with his many chewtoys.

If your dog does not eliminate within the allotted time outside—no biggie! Back to his doggy den, and then try again after another hour.

As I own large dogs, I always feel more relaxed walking an empty dog, knowing that I will not need to finish our stroll weighted down with bags of feces! Beware of falling into the trap of walking the dog to get it to eliminate. The good ol' dog walk is such an enormous highlight in the dog's life that it represents the single biggest potential reward in domestic dogdom. However, when in a hurry, or during inclement weather, many owners abruptly terminate the walk the moment the dog has done its business. This, in effect, severely punishes the dog for doing the right thing, in the right place at the right time. Consequently, many dogs become strongly inhibited from eliminating outdoors because they know it will signal an abrupt end to an otherwise thoroughly enjoyable walk.

Instead, instruct the dog to relieve himself in the yard prior to going for a walk. If you follow the above instructions, most dogs soon learn to eliminate on cue. As soon as the dog eliminates, praise (and offer a treat or two)—"Good dog! Let's go walkies!" Use the walk as a reward for eliminating in the yard. If the dog does not go, put him back in his doggy den and think about a walk later on. You will find with a "No feces–no walk" policy, your dog will become one of the fastest defecators in the business.

If you do not have a back yard, instruct the dog to eliminate right outside your front door prior to the walk. Not only will this facilitate clean up and disposal of the feces in your own trash can but, also, the walk may again be used as a colossal reward.

CHEWING AND BARKING

Short-term close confinement also teaches the dog that occasional quiet moments are a reality of domestic living. Your puppydog is extremely impressionable during his first few weeks at home. Regular

confinement at this time soon exerts a calming influ-
ence over the dog's personality. Remember, once the
dog is housetrained and calmer, there will be a whole
lifetime ahead for the dog to enjoy full run of the
house and garden. On the other hand, by letting the
newcomer have unrestricted access to the entire household and allowing him to run willy-nilly, he will most
certainly develop a bunch of behavior problems in
short order, no doubt necessitating confinement later
in life. It would not be fair to remedially restrain and
confine a dog you have trained, through neglect, to
run free.

When confining the dog, make sure he always has an
impressive array of suitable chewtoys. Kongs and sterilized longbones (both readily available from pet stores)
make the best chewtoys, since they are hollow and may
be stuffed with treats to heighten the dog's interest.
For example, by stuffing the little hole at the top of a
Kong with a small piece of freeze-dried liver, the dog
will not want to leave it alone.

Remember, treats do not have to be junk food and they
certainly should not represent extra calories. Rather,
treats should be part of each dog's regular daily diet:

Some food may be
served in the dog's
bowl for breakfast and
dinner, some food
may be used as train-
ing treats, and some
food may be used for
stuffing chewtoys. I
regularly stuff my
dogs' many Kongs
with different shaped
biscuits and kibble.

*Make sure your
puppy has suit-
able chewtoys.*

The kibble seems to fall out fairly easily, as do the
oval-shaped biscuits, thus rewarding the dog instanta-
neously for checking out the chewtoys. The bone-
shaped biscuits fall out after a while, rewarding the dog
for worrying at the chewtoy. But the triangular biscuits
never come out. They remain inside the Kong as lures,

maintaining the dog's fascination with its chewtoy. To further focus the dog's interest, I always make sure to flavor the triangular biscuits by rubbing them with a little cheese or freeze-dried liver.

If stuffed chewtoys are reserved especially for times the dog is confined, the puppy-dog will soon learn to enjoy quiet moments in her doggy den and she will quickly develop a chewtoy habit—a good habit! This is a simple *passive training* process; all the owner has to do is set up the situation and the dog all but trains herself—easy and effective. Even when the dog is given run of the house, her first inclination will be to indulge her rewarding chewtoy habit rather than destroying less-attractive household articles, such as curtains, carpets, chairs and compact disks. Similarly, a chewtoy chewer will be less inclined to scratch and chew herself excessively. Also, if the dog busies herself as a recreational chewer, she will be less inclined to develop into a recreational barker or digger when left at home alone.

Stuff a number of chewtoys whenever the dog is left confined and remove the extra-special-tasting treats when you return. Your dog will now amuse himself with his chewtoys before falling asleep and then resume playing with his chewtoys when he expects you to return. Since most owner-absent misbehavior happens right after you leave and right before your expected return, your puppydog will now be conveniently preoccupied with his chewtoys at these times.

To teach come, call your dog, open your arms as a welcoming signal, wave a toy or a treat and praise for every step in your direction.

Come and Sit

Most puppies will happily approach virtually anyone, whether called or not; that is, until they collide with adolescence and develop other more important doggy interests, such as sniffing a multiplicity of exquisite odors on the grass. Your mission, Mr. and/or Ms. Owner, is to teach and reward the pup for coming reliably, willingly and happily when called—and you have just three months to get it done. Unless adequately reinforced, your puppy's tendency to approach people will self-destruct by adolescence.

Call your dog ("Fido, come!"), open your arms (and maybe squat down) as a welcoming signal, waggle a treat or toy as a lure, and reward the puppydog when he comes running. Do not wait to praise the dog until he reaches you—he may come 95 percent of the way and then run off after some distraction. Instead, praise the dog's *first* step towards you and continue praising enthusiastically for *every* step he takes in your direction.

When the rapidly approaching puppy dog is three lengths away from impact, instruct him to sit ("Fido, sit!") and hold the lure in front of you in an outstretched hand to prevent him from hitting you mid-chest and knocking you flat on your back! As Fido decelerates to nose the lure, move the treat upwards and backwards just over his muzzle with an upwards motion of your extended arm (palm-upwards). As the dog looks up to follow the lure, he will sit down (if he jumps up, you are holding the lure too high). Praise the dog for sitting. Move backwards and call him again. Repeat this many times over, always praising when Fido comes and sits; on occasion, reward him.

For the first couple of trials, use a training treat both as a lure to entice the dog to come and sit and as a reward for doing so. Thereafter, try to use different items as lures and rewards. For example, lure the dog with a Kong or Frisbee but reward her with a food treat. Or lure the dog with a food treat but pat her and throw a tennis ball as a reward. After just a few repetitions, dispense with the lures and rewards; the dog will begin to respond willingly to your verbal requests and hand signals just for the prospect of praise from your heart and affection from your hands.

Instruct every family member, friend and visitor how to get the dog to come and sit. Invite people over for a series of pooch parties; do not keep the pup a secret— let other people enjoy this puppy, and let the pup enjoy other people. Puppydog parties are not only fun, they easily attract a lot of people to help *you* train *your* dog. Unless you teach your dog *how* to meet people, that is, to sit for greetings, no doubt the dog will resort to jumping up. Then you and the visitors will get annoyed, and the dog will be punished. This is not fair. *Send out those invitations for puppy parties and teach your dog to be mannerly and socially acceptable.*

Even though your dog quickly masters obedient recalls in the house, his reliability may falter when playing in the back yard or local park. Ironically, it is *the owner* who has unintentionally trained the dog *not* to respond in these instances. By allowing the dog to play and run around and otherwise have a good time, but then to call the dog to put him on leash to take him home, the dog quickly learns playing is fun but training is a drag. Thus, playing in the park becomes a severe distraction, which works against training. Bad news!

Instead, whether playing with the dog off leash or on leash, request him to come at frequent intervals— say, every minute or so. On most occasions, praise and pet the dog for a few seconds while he is sitting, then tell him to go play again. For especially fast recalls, offer a couple of training treats and take the time to praise and pet the dog enthusiastically before releasing him. The dog will learn that coming when called is not necessarily the end of the play session, and neither is it the end of the world; rather, it signals an enjoyable, quality time-out with the owner before resuming play once more. In fact, playing in the park now becomes a very effective life-reward, which works to facilitate training by reinforcing each obedient and timely recall. Good news!

Sit, Down, Stand and Rollover

Teaching the dog a variety of body positions is easy for owner and dog, impressive for spectators and extremely useful for all. Using lure-reward techniques, it is possible to train several positions at once to verbal commands or hand signals (which impress the socks off onlookers).

Sit and *down*—the two control commands—prevent or resolve nearly a hundred behavior problems. For example, if the dog happily and obediently sits or lies down when requested, he cannot jump on visitors, dash out the front door, run around and chase its tail, pester other dogs, harass cats or annoy family, friends or strangers. Additionally, "sit" or "down" are better emergency commands for off-leash control.

It is easier to teach and maintain a reliable sit than maintain a reliable recall. *Sit* is the purest and simplest of commands—either the dog is sitting or he is not. If there is any change of circumstances or potential danger in the park, for example, simply instruct the dog to sit. If he sits, you have a number of options: allow the dog to resume playing when he is safe; walk up and put the dog on leash, or call the dog. The dog will be much more likely to come when called if he has already acknowledged his compliance by sitting. If the dog does not sit in the park—train him to!

Stand and *rollover-stay* are the two positions for examining the dog. Your veterinarian will love you to distraction if you take a little time to teach the dog to stand still and roll over and play possum. Also, your vet bills will be smaller. The rollover-stay is an especially useful command and is really just a variation of the down-stay: whereas the dog lies prone in the traditional down, she lies supine in the rollover-stay.

As with teaching come and sit, the training techniques to teach the dog to assume all other body positions on cue are user-friendly and dog-friendly. Simply give the appropriate request, lure the dog into the desired body position using a training treat or toy and then *praise* (and maybe reward) the dog as soon as he complies. Try not to touch the dog to get him to respond. If you teach the dog by guiding him into position, the dog will quickly learn that rump-pressure means sit, for example, but as yet you still have no control over your dog if he is just six feet away. It will still be necessary to teach the dog to sit on request. So do not make training a time-consuming two-step process; instead, teach the dog to sit to a verbal request or hand signal from the outset. Once the dog sits willingly when requested, by all means use your hands to pet the dog when he does so.

To teach *down* when the dog is already sitting, say "Fido, down!," hold the lure in one hand (palm down) and lower that hand to the floor between the dog's forepaws. As the dog lowers his head to follow the lure, slowly move the lure away from the dog just a fraction (in front of his paws). The dog will lie down as he stretches his nose forward to follow the lure. Praise the dog when he does so. If the dog stands up, you pulled the lure away too far and too quickly.

When teaching the dog to lie down from the standing position, say "down" and lower the lure to the floor as before. Once the dog has lowered his forequarters and assumed a play bow, gently and slowly move the lure *towards* the dog between his forelegs. Praise the dog as soon as his rear end plops down.

After just a couple of trials it will be possible to alternate sits and downs and have the dog energetically perform doggy push-ups. Praise the dog a lot, and after half a dozen or so push-ups reward the dog with a training treat or toy. You will notice the more energetically you move your arm—upwards (palm up) to get the dog to sit, and downwards (palm down) to get the dog to lie down—the more energetically the dog responds to your requests. Now try training the dog in silence and you will notice he has also learned to respond to hand signals. Yeah! Not too shabby for the first session.

To teach *stand* from the sitting position, say "Fido, stand," slowly move the lure half a dog-length away from the dog's nose, keeping it at nose level, and praise the dog as he stands to follow the lure. As soon

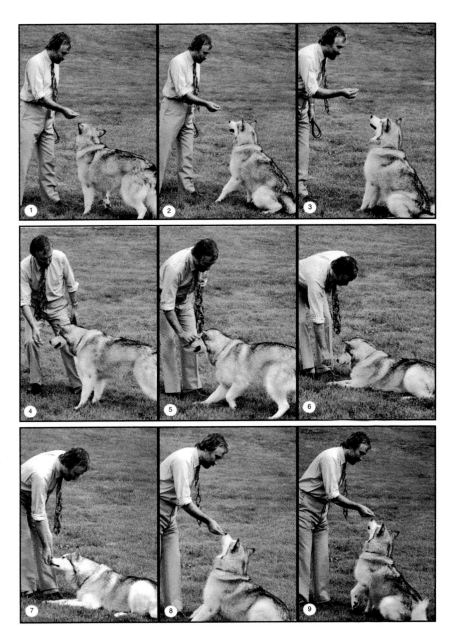

Using a food lure to teach sit, down and stand. 1) "Phoenix, Sit." 2) Hand palm upwards, move lure up and back over dog's muzzle. 3) "Good sit, Phoenix!" 4) "Phoenix, down." 5) Hand palm downwards, move lure down to lie between dog's forepaws. 6) "Phoenix, off. Good down, Phoenix!" 7) "Phoenix, sit!" 8) Palm upwards, move lure up and back, keeping it close to dog's muzzle. 9) "Good sit, Phoenix!"

10) *"Phoenix, stand!"* 11) *Move lure away from dog at nose height, then lower it a tad.* 12) *"Phoenix, off! Good stand, Phoenix!"* 13) *"Phoenix, down!"* 14) *Hand palm downwards, move lure down to lie between dog's forepaws.* 15) *"Phoenix, off! Good down-stay, Phoenix!"* 16) *"Phoenix, stand!"* 17) *Move lure away from dog's muzzle up to nose height.* 18) *"Phoenix, off! Good stand-stay, Phoenix. Now we'll make the vet and groomer happy!"*

as the dog stands, lower the lure to just beneath the dog's chin to entice him to look down; otherwise he will stand and then sit immediately. To prompt the dog to stand from the down position, move the lure half a dog-length upwards and away from the dog, holding the lure at standing nose height from the floor.

Teaching *rollover* is best started from the down position, with the dog lying on one side, or at least with both hind legs stretched out on the same side. Say "Fido, bang!" and move the lure backwards and alongside the dog's muzzle to its elbow (on the side of its outstretched hind legs). Once the dog looks to the side and backwards, very slowly move the lure upwards to the dog's shoulder and backbone. Tickling the dog in the goolies (groin area) often invokes a reflex-raising of the hind leg as an appeasement gesture, which facilitates the tendency to roll over. If you move the lure too quickly and the dog jumps into the standing position, have patience and start again. As soon as the dog rolls onto its back, keep the lure stationary and mesmerize the dog with a relaxing tummy rub.

To teach *rollover-stay* when the dog is standing or moving, say "Fido, bang!" and give the appropriate hand signal (with index finger pointed and thumb cocked in true Sam Spade fashion), then in one fluid movement lure him to first lie down and then rollover-stay as above.

Teaching the dog to *stay* in each of the above four positions becomes a piece of cake after first teaching the dog not to worry at the toy or treat training lure. This is best accomplished by hand feeding dinner kibble. Hold a piece of kibble firmly in your hand and softly instruct "Off!" Ignore any licking and slobbering *for however long the dog worries at the treat,* but say "Take it!" and offer the kibble *the instant* the dog breaks contact with his muzzle. Repeat this a few times, and then up the ante and insist the dog remove his muzzle for one whole second before offering the kibble. Then progressively refine your criteria and have the dog not touch your hand (or treat) for longer and longer periods on each trial, such as for two seconds, four seconds, then six, ten, fifteen, twenty, thirty seconds and so on. The dog soon learns: (1) worrying at the treat never gets results, whereas (2) noncontact is often rewarded after a variable time lapse.

Teaching *"Off!"* has many useful applications in its own right. Additionally, instructing the dog not to touch a training lure often produces spontaneous and magical stays. Request the dog to stand-stay, for example, and not to touch the lure. At first set your sights on a short two-second stay before rewarding the dog. (Remember, every long journey begins with a single step.) However, on subsequent trials, gradually and progressively increase the length of stay required to receive a reward. In no time at all your dog will stand calmly for a minute or so.

Relevancy Training

Once you have taught the dog what you expect her to do when requested to come, sit, lie down, stand, rollover and stay, the time is right to teach the dog *why* she should comply with your wishes. The secret is to have many (*many*) extremely short training interludes (two to five seconds each) at numerous (*numerous*) times during the course of the dog's day. Especially work with the dog immediately *before* the dog's good times and *during* the dog's good times. For example, ask your dog to sit and/or lie down each time before opening doors, serving meals, offering treats and tummy rubs; ask the dog to perform a few controlled doggy push-ups before letting her off-leash or throwing a tennis ball; and perhaps request the dog to sit-down-sit-stand-down-stand-rollover before inviting her to cuddle on the couch.

Similarly, request the dog to sit many times during play or on walks, and in no time at all the dog will be only too pleased to follow your instructions because he has learned that a compliant response heralds all sorts of goodies. Basically all you are trying to teach the dog is how to say please: "Please throw the tennis ball. Please may I snuggle on the couch."

Remember, whereas it is important to keep training interludes short, it is equally important to have many short sessions each and every day. The shortest (and most useful) session comprises asking the dog to sit and then go play during a play session. When trained this way, your dog will soon associate training with good times. In fact, the dog may be unable to distinguish between training and good times and, indeed, there should be no distinction. The warped concept that training involves forcing the dog to comply and/or dominating his will is totally at odds with the picture of a truly well-trained dog. In reality, enjoying a game of training with a dog is no different from enjoying a game of backgammon or tennis with a friend; and walking with a dog should be no different from strolling with buddies on the golf course.

Walk by Your Side

Many people attempt to teach a dog to heel by putting him on a leash and physically correcting the dog when he makes mistakes. There are a number of things seriously wrong with this approach, the first being that most people do not want precision heeling; rather, they simply want the dog to follow or walk by their side. Second, when physically restrained during "training," even though the dog may grudgingly mope by your side when "handcuffed" on leash, let's see what happens when he is off leash. History! The dog is in the next county because he never enjoyed walking with you on leash and you have no control over him off leash. So let's just teach the dog off leash from the outset to *want* to walk with us. Third, if the dog has not been trained to heel, it is a trifle hasty to think about punishing the poor dog for making mistakes and breaking heeling rules he didn't even know existed. This is simply not fair! Surely, if the dog had been adequately taught how to heel, he would seldom make mistakes and hence there would be no need to correct the dog. Remember, each mistake and each correction (punishment) advertise the trainer's inadequacy, not the dog's. The dog is not stubborn, he is not stupid and he is not bad. Even if he were, he would still require training, so let's train him properly.

Let's teach the dog to *enjoy* following us and to *want* to walk by our side offleash. Then it will be easier to teach high-precision off-leash heeling patterns if desired. After attaching the leash for safety on outdoor walks, but before going anywhere, it is necessary to teach the dog specifically not to pull. Now it will be much easier to teach on-leash walking and heeling because the dog already wants to walk with you, he is familiar with the desired walking and heeling positions and he knows not to pull.

FOLLOWING

Start by training your dog to follow you. Many puppies will follow if you simply walk away from them and maybe click your fingers or chuckle. Adult dogs may require additional enticement to stimulate them to follow, such as a training lure or, at the very least, a lively trainer. To teach the dog to follow: (1) keep walking and (2) walk away from the dog. If the dog attempts to lead or lag, change pace; slow down if the dog forges too far ahead, but speed up if he lags too far behind. Say "Steady!" or "Easy!" each time before you slow down and "Quickly!" or "Hustle!" each time before you speed up, and the dog will learn to change pace on cue. If the dog lags or leads too far, or if he wanders right or left, simply walk quickly in the opposite direction and maybe even run away from the dog and hide.

Practicing is a lot of fun; you can set up a course in your home, yard or park to do this. Indoors, entice the dog to follow upstairs, into a bedroom, into the bathroom, downstairs, around the living room couch, zigzagging between dining room chairs and into the kitchen for dinner. Outdoors, get the dog to follow around park benches, trees, shrubs and along walkways and lines in the grass. (For safety outdoors, it is advisable to attach a long line on the dog, but never exert corrective tension on the line.)

Remember, following has a lot to do with attitude—
your attitude! Most probably your dog will *not* want to
follow Mr. Grumpy Troll with the personality of wilted
lettuce. Lighten up—walk with a jaunty step, whistle a
happy tune, sing, skip and tell jokes to your dog and he
will be right there by your side.

BY YOUR SIDE

It is smart to train the dog to walk close on one side or
the other—either side will do, your choice. When walking, jogging or cycling, it is generally bad news to have
the dog suddenly cut in front of you. In fact, I train my
dogs to walk "By my side" and "Other side"—both very
useful instructions. It is possible to position the dog
fairly accurately by looking to the appropriate side and
clicking your fingers or slapping your thigh on that
side. A precise positioning may be attained by holding
a training lure, such as a chewtoy, tennis ball, or food
treat. Stop and stand still several times throughout the
walk, just as you would when window shopping or
meeting a friend. Use the lure to make sure the dog
slows down and stays close whenever you stop.

When teaching the dog to heel, we generally want
her to sit in heel position when we stop. Teach heel

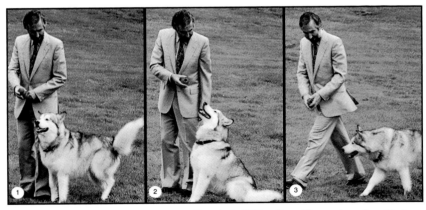

*Using a toy to teach sit-heel-sit sequences: 1) "Phoenix, heel!" Standing still, move lure up and back
over dog's muzzle.... 2) To position dog sitting in heel position on your left side. 3) "Phoenix, heel!"
wagging lure in left hand. Change lure to right hand in preparation for sit signal.*

position at the standstill and the dog will learn that the default heel position is sitting by your side (left or right—your choice, unless you wish to compete in obedience trials, in which case the dog must heel on the left).

Several times a day, stand up and call your dog to come and sit in heel position—"Fido, heel!" For example, instruct the dog to come to heel each time there are commercials on TV, or each time you turn a page of a novel, and the dog will get it in a single evening.

Practice straight-line heeling and turns separately. With the dog sitting at heel, teach him to turn in place. After each quarter-turn, half-turn or full turn in place, lure the dog to sit at heel. Now it's time for short straight-line heeling sequences, no more than a few steps at a time. Always think of heeling in terms of Sit-Heel-Sit sequences—start and end with the dog in position and do your best to keep him there when moving. Progressively increase the number of steps in each sequence. When the dog remains close for 20 yards of straight-line heeling, it is time to add a few turns and then sign up for a happy-heeling obedience class to get some advice from the experts.

4) Use hand signal only to lure dog to sit as you stop. Eventually, dog will sit automatically at heel whenever you stop. 5) "Good dog!"

NO PULLING ON LEASH

You can start teaching your dog not to pull on leash anywhere—in front of the television or outdoors—but regardless of location, you must not take a single step with tension in the leash. For a reason known only to dogs, even just a couple of paces of pulling on leash is intrinsically motivating and diabolically rewarding. Instead, attach the leash to the dog's collar, grasp the other end firmly with both hands held close to your chest, and stand still—do not budge an inch. Have somebody watch you with a stopwatch to time your progress, or else you will never believe this will work and so you will not even try the exercise, and your shoulder and the dog's neck will be traumatized for years to come.

Stand still and wait for the dog to stop pulling, and to sit and/or lie down. All dogs stop pulling and sit eventually. Most take only a couple of minutes; the all-time record is 22 1/5 minutes. Time how long it takes. Gently praise the dog when he stops pulling, and as soon as he sits, enthusiastically praise the dog and take just one step forwards, then immediately stand still. This single step usually demonstrates the ballistic reinforcing nature of pulling on leash; most dogs explode to the end of the leash, so be prepared for the strain. Stand firm and wait for the dog to sit again. Repeat this half a dozen times and you will probably notice a progressive reduction in the force of the dog's one-step explosions and a radical reduction in the time it takes for the dog to sit each time.

As the dog learns "Sit we go" and "Pull we stop," she will begin to walk forward calmly with each single step and automatically sit when you stop. Now try two steps before you stop. Wooooooo! Scary! When the dog has mastered two steps at a time, try for three. After each success, progressively increase the number of steps in the sequence: try four steps and then six, eight, ten and twenty steps before stopping. Congratulations! You are now walking the dog on leash.

Whenever walking with the dog (off leash or on leash), make sure you stop periodically to practice a few position commands and stays before instructing the dog to "Walk on!" (Remember, you want the dog to be compliant everywhere, not just in the kitchen when his dinner is at hand.) For example, stopping every 25 yards to briefly train the dog amounts to over 200 training interludes within a single three-mile stroll. And each training session is in a different location. You will not believe the improvement within just the first mile of the first walk.

To put it another way, integrating training into a walk offers 200 separate opportunities to use the continuance of the walk as a reward to reinforce the dog's education. Moreover, some training interludes may comprise continuing education for the dog's walking skills: Alternate short periods of the dog walking calmly by your side with periods when the dog is allowed to sniff and investigate the environment. Now sniffing odors on the grass and meeting other dogs become rewards which reinforce the dog's calm and mannerly demeanor. Good Lord! Whatever next? Many enjoyable walks together of course. Happy trails!

THE IMPORTANCE OF TRICKS

Nothing will improve a dog's quality of life better than having a few tricks under its belt. Teaching any trick expands the dog's vocabulary, which facilitates communication and improves the owner's control. Also, specific tricks help prevent and resolve specific behavior problems. For example, by teaching the dog to fetch his toys, the dog learns carrying a toy makes the owner happy and, therefore, will be more likely to chew his toy than other inappropriate items.

More important, teaching tricks prompts owners to lighten up and train with a sunny disposition. Really, tricks should be no different from any other behaviors we put on cue. But they are. When teaching tricks, owners have a much sweeter attitude, which in turn motivates the dog and improves her willingness to comply. The dog feels tricks are a blast, but formal commands are a drag. In fact, tricks are so enjoyable, they may be used as rewards in training by asking the dog to come, sit and down-stay and then rollover for a tummy rub. Go on, try it: Crack a smile and even giggle when the dog promptly and willingly lies down and stays.

Most important, performing tricks prompts onlookers to smile and giggle. Many people are scared of dogs, especially large ones. And nothing can be more off-putting for a dog than to be constantly confronted by strangers who don't like him because of his size or the way he looks. Uneasy people put the dog on edge, causing him to back off and bark, only frightening people all the more. And so a vicious circle develops, with the people's fear fueling the dog's fear *and vice versa*. Instead, tie a pink ribbon to your dog's collar and practice all sorts of tricks on walks and in the park, and you will be pleasantly amazed how it changes people's attitudes toward your friendly dog. The dog's repertoire of tricks is limited only by the trainer's imagination. Below I have described three of my favorites:

SPEAK AND SHUSH

The training sequence involved in teaching a dog to bark on request is no different from that used when training any behavior on cue: request—lure—response—reward. As always, the secret of success lies in finding an effective lure. If the dog always barks at the doorbell, for example, say "Rover, speak!", have an accomplice ring the doorbell, then reward the dog for barking. After a few woofs, ask Rover to "Shush!", waggle a food treat under his nose (to entice him to sniff and thus to shush), praise him when quiet and eventually offer the treat as a reward. Alternate "Speak" and "Shush," progressively increasing the length of shush-time between each barking bout.

PLAYBOW

With the dog standing, say "Bow!" and lower the food lure (palm upwards) to rest between the dog's forepaws. Praise as the dog lowers

her forequarters and sternum to the ground (as when teaching the down), but then lure the dog to stand and offer the treat. On successive trials, gradually increase the length of time the dog is required to remain in the playbow posture in order to gain a food reward. If the dog's rear end collapses into a down, say nothing and offer no reward; simply start over.

BE A BEAR

With the dog sitting backed into a corner to prevent him from toppling over backwards, say "Be a Bear!" With bent paw and palm down, raise a lure upwards and backwards along the top of the dog's muzzle. Praise the dog when he sits up on his haunches and offer the treat as a reward. To prevent the dog from standing on his hind legs, keep the lure closer to the dog's muzzle. On each trial, progressively increase the length of time the dog is required to sit up to receive a food reward. Since lure/reward training is so easy, teach the dog to stand and walk on his hind legs as well!

Teaching "Be a Bear"

chapter 9

Getting
Active
with your Dog

by Bardi McLennan

Once you and your dog have graduated from basic obedience training and are beginning to work together as a team, you can take part in the growing world of dog activities. There are so many fun things to do with your dog! Just remember, people and dogs don't always learn at the same pace, so don't be upset if you (or your dog) need more than two basic training courses before your team becomes operational. Even smart dogs don't go straight to college from kindergarten!

Just as there are events geared to certain types of dogs, so there are ones that are more appealing to certain types of people. In some

128

activities, you give the commands and your dog does the work (upland game hunting is one example), while in others, such as agility, you'll both get a workout. You may want to aim for prestigious titles to add to your dog's name, or you may want nothing more than the sheer enjoyment of being around other people and their dogs. Passive or active, participation has its own rewards.

Consider your dog's physical capabilities when looking into any of the canine activities. It's easy to see that a Basset Hound is not built for the racetrack, nor would a Chihuahua be the breed of choice for pulling a sled. A loyal dog will attempt almost anything you ask him to do, so it is up to you to know your dog's limitations. A dog must be physically sound in order to compete at any level in athletic activities, and being mentally sound is a definite plus. Advanced age, however, may not be a deterrent. Many dogs still hunt and herd at ten or twelve years of age. It's entirely possible for dogs to be "fit at 50." Take your dog for a checkup, explain to your vet the type of activity you have in mind and be guided by his or her findings.

All dogs seem to love playing flyball.

You needn't be restricted to breed-specific sports if it's only fun you're after. Certain AKC activities are limited to designated breeds; however, as each new trial, test or sport has grown in popularity, so has the variety of breeds encouraged to participate at a fun level.

But don't shortchange your fun, or that of your dog, by thinking only of the basic function of her breed. Once a dog has learned how to learn, she can be taught to do just about anything as long as the size of the dog is right for the job and you both think it is fun and rewarding. In other words, you are a team.

129

To get involved in any of the activities detailed in this chapter, look for the names and addresses of the organizations that sponsor them in Chapter 13. You can also ask your breeder or a local dog trainer for contacts.

You can compete in obedience trials with a well trained dog.

Official American Kennel Club Activities

The following tests and trials are some of the events sanctioned by the AKC and sponsored by various dog clubs. Your dog's expertise will be rewarded with impressive titles. You can participate just for fun, or be competitive and go for those awards.

OBEDIENCE

Training classes begin with pups as young as three months of age in kindergarten puppy training, then advance to pre-novice (all exercises on lead) and go on to novice, which is where you'll start off-lead work. In obedience classes dogs learn to sit, stay, heel and come through a variety of exercises. Once you've got the basics down, you can enter obedience trials and work toward earning your dog's first degree, a C.D. (Companion Dog).

The next level is called "Open," in which jumps and retrieves perk up the dog's interest. Passing grades in competition at this level earn a C.D.X. (Companion Dog Excellent). Beyond that lies the goal of the most ambitious—Utility (U.D. and even U.D.X. or OTCh, an Obedience Champion).

AGILITY

All dogs can participate in the latest canine sport to have gained worldwide popularity for its fun and excitement, agility. It began in England as a canine version of horse show-jumping, but because dogs are more agile and able to perform on verbal commands, extra feats were added such as climbing, balancing and racing through tunnels or in and out of weave poles. Many of the obstacles (regulation or homemade) can be set up in your own backyard. If the agility bug bites, you could end up in international competition!

For starters, your dog should be obedience trained, even though, in the beginning, the lessons may all be taught on lead. Once the dog understands the commands (and you do, too), it's as easy as guiding the dog over a prescribed course, one obstacle at a time. In competition, the race is against the clock, so wear your running shoes! The dog starts with 200 points and the judge deducts for infractions and misadventures along the way.

All dogs seem to love agility and respond to it as if they were being turned loose in a playground paradise. Your dog's enthusiasm will be contagious; agility turns into great fun for dog and owner.

FIELD TRIALS AND HUNTING TESTS

There are field trials and hunting tests for the sporting breeds—retrievers, spaniels and pointing breeds, and for some hounds—Bassets, Beagles and Dachshunds. Field trials are competitive events that test a dog's ability to perform the functions for which she was bred. Hunting tests, which are open to retrievers,

---

TITLES AWARDED BY THE AKC

Conformation: Ch. (Champion)

Obedience: CD (Companion Dog); CDX (Companion Dog Excellent); UD (Utility Dog); UDX (Utility Dog Excellent); OTCh. (Obedience Trial Champion)

Field: JH (Junior Hunter); SH (Senior Hunter); MH (Master Hunter); AFCh. (Amateur Field Champion); FCh. (Field Champion)

Lure Coursing: JC (Junior Courser); SC (Senior Courser)

Herding: HT (Herding Tested); PT (Pre-Trial Tested); HS (Herding Started); HI (Herding Intermediate); HX (Herding Excellent); HCh. (Herding Champion)

Tracking: TD (Tracking Dog); TDX (Tracking Dog Excellent)

Agility: NAD (Novice Agility); OAD (Open Agility); ADX (Agility Excellent); MAX (Master Agility)

Earthdog Tests: JE (Junior Earthdog); SE (Senior Earthdog); ME (Master Earthdog)

Canine Good Citizen: CGC

Combination: DC (Dual Champion—Ch. and Fch.); TC (Triple Champion—Ch., Fch., and OTCh.)

---

spaniels and pointing breeds only, are noncompetitive and are a means of judging the dog's ability as well as that of the handler.

Hunting is a very large and complex part of canine sports, and if you own one of the breeds that hunts, the events are a great treat for your dog and you. He gets to do what he was bred for, and you get to work with him and watch him do it. You'll be proud of and amazed at what your dog can do.

Fortunately, the AKC publishes a series of booklets on these events, which outline the rules and regulations and include a glossary of the sometimes complicated terms. The AKC also publishes newsletters for field trialers and hunting test enthusiasts. The United Kennel Club (UKC) also has informative materials for the hunter and his dog.

Retrievers and other sporting breeds get to do what they're bred to in hunting tests.

HERDING TESTS AND TRIALS

Herding, like hunting, dates back to the first known uses man made of dogs. The interest in herding today is widespread, and if you own a herding breed, you can join in the activity. Herding dogs are tested for their natural skills to keep a flock of ducks, sheep or cattle together. If your dog shows potential, you can start at the testing level, where your dog can earn a title for showing an inherent herding ability. With training you can advance to the trial level, where your dog should be capable of controlling even difficult livestock in diverse situations.

LURE COURSING

The AKC Tests and Trials for Lure Coursing are open to traditional sighthounds—Greyhounds, Whippets,

Borzoi, Salukis, Afghan Hounds, Ibizan Hounds and Scottish Deerhounds—as well as to Basenjis and Rhodesian Ridgebacks. Hounds are judged on overall ability, follow, speed, agility and endurance. This is possibly the most exciting of the trials for spectators, because the speed and agility of the dogs is awesome to watch as they chase the lure (or "course") in heats of two or three dogs at a time.

Tracking

Tracking is another activity in which almost any dog can compete because every dog that sniffs the ground when taken outdoors is, in fact, tracking. The hard part comes when the rules as to what, when and where the dog tracks are determined by a person, not the dog! Tracking tests cover a large area of fields, woods and roads. The tracks are laid hours before the dogs go to work on them, and include "tricks" like cross-tracks and sharp turns. If you're interested in search-and-rescue work, this is the place to start.

This tracking dog is hot on the trail.

Earthdog Tests for Small Terriers and Dachshunds

These tests are open to Australian, Bedlington, Border, Cairn, Dandie Dinmont, Smooth and Wire Fox, Lakeland, Norfolk, Norwich, Scottish, Sealyham, Skye, Welsh and West Highland White Terriers as well as Dachshunds. The dogs need no prior training for this terrier sport. There is a qualifying test on the day of the event, so dog and handler learn the rules on the spot. These tests, or "digs," sometimes end with informal races in the late afternoon.

Here are some of the extracurricular obedience and racing activities that are not regulated by the AKC or UKC, but are generally run by clubs or a group of dog fanciers and are often open to all.

Canine Freestyle This activity is something new on the scene and is variously likened to dancing, dressage or ice skating. It is meant to show the athleticism of the dog, but also requires showmanship on the part of the dog's handler. If you and your dog like to ham it up for friends, you might want to look into freestyle.

Lure coursing lets sighthounds do what they do best—run!

Scent Hurdle Racing Scent hurdle racing is purely a fun activity sponsored by obedience clubs with members forming competing teams. The height of the hurdles is based on the size of the shortest dog on the team. On a signal, one team dog is released on each of two side-by-side courses and must clear every hurdle before picking up its own dumbbell from a platform and returning over the jumps to the handler. As each dog returns, the next on that team is sent. Of course, that is what the dogs are supposed to do. When the dogs improvise (going under or around the hurdles, stealing another dog's dumbbell, and so forth), it no doubt frustrates the handlers, but just adds to the fun for everyone else.

Flyball This type of racing is similar, but after negotiating the four hurdles, the dog comes to a flyball box, steps on a lever that releases a tennis ball into the air, catches the ball and returns over the hurdles to the starting point. This game also becomes extremely fun for spectators because the dogs sometimes cheat by catching a ball released by the dog in the next lane. Three titles can be earned—Flyball Dog (F.D.), Flyball Dog Excellent (F.D.X.) and Flyball Dog Champion (Fb.D.Ch.)—all awarded by the North American Flyball Association, Inc.

Dogsledding The name conjures up the Rocky Mountains or the frigid North, but you can find dogsled clubs in such unlikely spots as Maryland, North Carolina and Virginia! Dogsledding is primarily for the Nordic breeds such as the Alaskan Malamutes, Siberian Huskies and Samoyeds, but other breeds can try. There are some practical backyard applications to this sport, too. With parental supervision, almost any strong dog could pull a child's sled.

Coming over the A-frame on an agility course.

These are just some of the many recreational ways you can get to know and understand your multifaceted dog better and have fun doing it.

Your Dog
and your
Family

by Bardi McLennan

Adding a dog automatically increases your family by one, no matter whether you live alone in an apartment or are part of a mother, father and six kids household. The single-person family is fair game for numerous and varied canine misconceptions as to who is dog and who pays the bills, whereas a dog in a houseful of children will consider himself to be just one of the gang, littermates all. One dog and one child may give a dog reason to believe they are both kids or both dogs.

Either interpretation requires parental supervision and sometimes speedy intervention.

As soon as one paw goes through the door into your home, Rufus (or Rufina) has to make many adjustments to become a part of your

136

family. Your job is to make him fit in as painlessly as possible. An older dog may have some frame of reference from past experience, but to a 10-week-old puppy, everything is brand new: people, furniture, stairs, when and where people eat, sleep or watch TV, his own place and everyone else's space, smells, sounds, outdoors—everything!

Puppies, and newly acquired dogs of any age, do not need what we think of as "freedom." If you leave a new dog or puppy loose in the house, you will almost certainly return to chaotic destruction and the dog will forever after equate your homecoming with a time of punishment to be dreaded. It is unfair to give your dog what amounts to "freedom to get into trouble." Instead, confine him to a crate for brief periods of your absence (up to three or four hours) and, for the long haul, a workday for example, confine him to one untrashable area with his own toys, a bowl of water and a radio left on (low) in another room.

*Lots of pets get
along with each
other just fine.*

For the first few days, when not confined, put Rufus on a long leash tied to your wrist or waist. This umbilical cord method enables the dog to learn all about you from your body language and voice, and to learn by his own actions which things in the house are NO! and which ones are rewarded by "Good dog." House-training will be easier with the pup always by your side. Speaking of which, accidents do happen. That goal of "completely housetrained" takes up to a year, or the length of time it takes the pup to mature.

The All-Adult Family

Most dogs in an adults-only household today are likely to be latchkey pets, with no one home all day but the dog. When you return after a tough day on the job, the dog can and should be your relaxation therapy. But going home can instead be a daily frustration.

Separation anxiety is a very common problem for the dog in a working household. It may begin with whines and barks of loneliness, but it will soon escalate into a frenzied destruction derby. That is why it is so important to set aside the time to teach a dog to relax when left alone in his confined area and to understand that he can trust you to return.

Let the dog get used to your work schedule in easy stages. Confine him to one room and go in and out of that room over and over again. Be casual about it. No physical, voice or eye contact. When the pup no longer even notices your comings and goings, leave the house for varying lengths of time, returning to stay home for a few minutes and gradually increasing the time away. This training can take days, but the dog is learning that you haven't left him forever and that he can trust you.

Any time you leave the dog, but especially during this training period, be casual about your departure. No anxiety-building fond farewells. Just "Bye" and go! Remember the "Good dog" when you return to find everything more or less as you left it.

If things are a mess (or even a disaster) when you return, greet the dog, take him outside to eliminate, and then put him in his crate while you clean up. Rant and rave in the shower! *Do not* punish the dog. You were not there when it happened, and the rule is: Only punish as you catch the dog in the act of wrongdoing. Obviously, it makes sense to get your latchkey puppy when you'll have a week or two to spend on these training essentials.

Family weekend activities should include Rufus whenever possible. Depending on the pup's age, now is the time for a long walk in the park, playtime in the backyard, a hike in the woods. Socializing is as important as health care, good food and physical exercise, so visiting Aunt Emma or Uncle Harry and the next-door neighbor's dog or cat is essential to developing an out-going, friendly temperament in your pet.

If you are a single adult, socializing Rufus at home and away will prevent him from becoming overly protective of you (or just overly attached) and will also prevent such behavioral problems as dominance or fear of strangers.

Babies

Whether already here or on the way, babies figure larger than life in the eyes of a dog. If the dog is there first, let him in on all your baby preparations in the house. When baby arrives, let Rufus sniff any item of clothing that has been on the baby before Junior comes home. Then let Mom greet the dog first before introducing the new family member. Hold the baby down for the dog to see and sniff, but make sure some-

one's holding the dog on lead in case of any sudden moves. Don't play keep-away or tease the dog with the baby, which only invites undesirable jumping up.

The dog and the baby are "family," and for starters can be treated almost as equals. Things rapidly change, however, especially when baby takes to creeping around on all fours on the dog's turf or, better yet, has yummy pudding all over her face

and hands! That's when a lot of things in the dog's and baby's lives become more separate than equal.

Dogs are perfect confidants.

Toddlers make terrible dog owners, but if you can't avoid the combination, use patient discipline (that is, positive teaching rather than punishment), and use time-outs before you run out of patience.

A dog and a baby (or toddler, or an assertive young child) should never be left alone together. Take the dog with you or confine him. With a baby or youngsters in the house, you'll have plenty of use for that wonderful canine safety device called a crate!

Young Children

Any dog in a house with kids will behave pretty much as the kids do, good or bad. But even good dogs and good children can get into trouble when play becomes rowdy and active.

Teach children how to play nicely with a puppy.

Legs bobbing up and down, shrill voices screeching, a ball hurtling overhead, all add up to exuberant frustration for a dog who's just trying to be part of the gang. In a pack of puppies, any legs or toys being chased would be caught by a set of teeth, and all the pups involved would understand that is how the game is played. Kids do not understand this, nor do parents tolerate it. Bring Rufus indoors before you have reason to regret it. This is time-out, not a punishment.

You can explain the situation to the children and tell them they must play quieter games until the puppy learns not to grab them with his mouth. Unfortunately, you can't explain it that easily to the dog. With adult supervision, they will learn how to play together.

Young children love to tease. Sticking their faces or wiggling their hands or fingers in the dog's face is teasing. To another person it might be just annoying, but it is threatening to a dog. There's another difference: We can make the child stop by an explanation, but the only way a dog can stop it is with a warning growl and then with teeth. Teasing is the major cause of children being bitten by their pets. Treat it seriously.

Older Children

The best age for a child to get a first dog is between the ages of 8 and 12. That's when kids are able to accept some real responsibility for their pet. Even so, take the child's vow of "I will never *ever* forget to feed (brush, walk, etc.) the dog" for what it's worth: a child's good intention at that moment. Most kids today have extra lessons, soccer practice, Little League, ballet, and so forth piled on top of school schedules. There will be many times when Mom will have to come to the dog's rescue. "I walked the dog for you so you can set the table for me" is one way to get around a missed appointment without laying on blame or guilt.

Kids in this age group make excellent obedience trainers because they are into the teaching/learning process themselves and they lack the self-consciousness of adults. Attending a dog show is something the whole family can enjoy, and watching Junior Showmanship may catch the eye of the kids. Older children can begin to get involved in many of the recreational activities that were reviewed in the previous chapter. Some of the agility obstacles, for example, can be set up in the backyard as a family project (with an adult making sure all the equipment is safe and secure for the dog).

Older kids are also beginning to look to the future, and may envision themselves as veterinarians or trainers or show dog handlers or writers of the next Lassie best-seller. Dogs are perfect confidants for these dreams. They won't tell a soul.

Other Pets

Introduce all pets tactfully. In a dog/cat situation, hold the dog, not the cat. Let two dogs meet on neutral turf—a stroll in the park or a walk down the street—with both on loose leads to permit all the normal canine ways of saying hello, including routine sniffing, circling, more sniffing, and so on. Small creatures such as hamsters, chinchillas or mice must be kept safe from their natural predators (dogs and cats).

Festive Family Occasions

Parties are great for people, but not necessarily for puppies. Until all the guests have arrived, put the dog in his crate or in a room where he won't be disturbed. A socialized dog can join the fun later as long as he's not underfoot, annoying guests or into the hors d'oeuvres.

There are a few dangers to consider, too. Doors opening and closing can allow a puppy to slip out unnoticed in the confusion, and you'll be organizing a search party instead of playing host or hostess. Party food and buffet service are not for dogs. Let Rufus party in his crate with a nice big dog biscuit.

At Christmas time, not only are tree decorations dangerous and breakable (and perhaps family heirlooms), but extreme caution should be taken with the lights, cords and outlets for the tree lights and any other festive lighting. Occasionally a dog lifts a leg, ignoring the fact that the tree is indoors. To avoid this, use a canine repellent, made for gardens, on the tree. Or keep him out of the tree room unless supervised. And whatever you do, *don't* invite trouble by hanging his toys on the tree!

Car Travel

Before you plan a vacation by car or RV with Rufus, be sure he enjoys car travel. Nothing spoils a holiday quicker than a carsick dog! Work within the dog's comfort level. Get in the car with the dog in his crate or attached to a canine car safety belt and just sit there until he relaxes. That's all. Next time, get in the car, turn on the engine and go nowhere. Just sit. When that is okay, turn on the engine and go around the block. Now you can go for a ride and include a stop where you get out, leaving the dog for a minute or two.

On a warm day, always park in the shade and leave windows open several inches. And return quickly. It only takes 10 minutes for a car to become an overheated steel death trap.

Motel or Pet Motel?

Not all motels or hotels accept pets, but you have a much better choice today than even a few years ago. To find a dog-friendly lodging, look at *On the Road Again With Man's Best Friend*, a series of directories that detail bed and breakfasts, inns, family resorts and other hotels/motels. Some places require a refundable deposit to cover any damage incurred by the dog. More B&Bs accept pets now, but some restrict the size.

If taking Rufus with you is not feasible, check out boarding kennels in your area. Your veterinarian may offer this service, or recommend a kennel or two he or she is familiar with. Go see the facilities for yourself, ask about exercise, diet, housing, and so on. Or, if you'd rather have Rufus stay home, look into bonded petsitters, many of whom will also bring in the mail and water your plants.

chapter 11

Your Dog
and your
Community

by Bardi McLennan

Step outside your home with your dog and you are no longer just family, you are both part of your community. This is when the phrase "responsible pet ownership" takes on serious implications. For starters, it means you pick up after your dog—not just occasionally, but every time your dog eliminates away from home. That means you have joined the Plastic Baggy Brigade! You always have plastic sandwich bags in your pocket and several in the car. It means you teach your kids how to use them, too. If you think this is "yucky," just imagine what the person (a non-doggy person) who inadvertently steps in the mess thinks!

Your responsibility extends to your neighbors: To their ears (no annoying barking); to their property (their garbage, their lawn, their flower beds, their cat—especially their cat); to their kids (on bikes, at play); to their kids' toys and sports equipment.

There are numerous dog-related laws, ranging from simple dog licensing and leash laws to those holding you liable for any physical injury or property damage done by your dog. These laws are in place to protect everyone in the community, including you and your dog. There are town ordinances and state laws which are by no means the same in all towns or all states. Ignorance of the law won't get you off the hook. The time to find out what the laws are where you live is now.

Be sure your dog's license is current. This is not just a good local ordinance, it can make the difference between finding your lost dog or not.

Dressing your dog up makes him appealing to strangers.

Many states now require proof of rabies vaccination and that the dog has been spayed or neutered before issuing a license. At the same time, keep up the dog's annual immunizations.

Never let your dog run loose in the neighborhood. This will not only keep you on the right side of the leash law, it's the outdoor version of the rule about not giving your dog "freedom to get into trouble."

Good Canine Citizen

Sometimes it's hard for a dog's owner to assess whether or not the dog is sufficiently socialized to be accepted by the community at large. Does Rufus or Rufina display good, controlled behavior in public? The AKC's Canine Good Citizen program is available through many dog organizations. If your dog passes the test, the title "CGC" is earned.

The overall purpose is to turn your dog into a good neighbor and to teach you about your responsibility to your community as a dog owner. Here are the ten things your dog must do willingly:

1. Accept a stranger stopping to chat with you.
2. Sit and be petted by a stranger.
3. Allow a stranger to handle him or her as a groomer or veterinarian would.
4. Walk nicely on a loose lead.
5. Walk calmly through a crowd.
6. Sit and down on command, then stay in a sit or down position while you walk away.
7. Come when called.
8. Casually greet another dog.
9. React confidently to distractions.
10. Accept being left alone with someone other than you and not become overly agitated or nervous.

Schools and Dogs

Schools are getting involved with pet ownership on an educational level. It has been proven that children who are kind to animals are humane in their attitude toward other people as adults.

A dog is a child's best friend, and so children are often primary pet owners, if not the primary caregivers. Unfortunately, they are also the ones most often bitten by dogs. This occurs due to a lack of understanding that pets, no matter how sweet, cuddly and loving, are still animals. Schools, along with parents, dog clubs, dog fanciers and the AKC, are working to change all that with video programs for children not only in grade school, but in the nursery school and pre-kindergarten age group. Teaching youngsters how to be responsible dog owners is important community work. When your dog has a CGC, volunteer to take part in an educational classroom event put on by your dog club.

Boy Scout Merit Badge

A Merit Badge for Dog Care can be earned by any Boy Scout ages 11 to 18. The requirements are not easy, but amount to a complete course in responsible dog care and general ownership. Here are just a few of the things a Scout must do to earn that badge:

Point out ten parts of the dog using the correct names.

Give a report (signed by parent or guardian) on your care of the dog (feeding, food used, housing, exercising, grooming and bathing), plus what has been done to keep the dog healthy.

Explain the right way to obedience train a dog, and demonstrate three comments.

Several of the requirements have to do with health care, including first aid, handling a hurt dog, and the dangers of home treatment for a serious ailment.

The final requirement is to know the local laws and ordinances involving dogs.

There are similar programs for Girl Scouts and 4-H members.

Local Clubs

Local dog clubs are no longer in existence just to put on a yearly dog show. Today, they are apt to be the hub of the community's involvement with pets. Dog clubs conduct educational forums with big-name speakers, stage demonstrations of canine talent in a busy mall and take dogs of various breeds to schools for class-room discussion.

The quickest way to feel accepted as a member in a club is to volunteer your services! Offer to help with something—anything—and watch your popularity (and your interest) grow.

Therapy Dogs

Once your dog has earned that essential CGC and reliably demonstrates a steady, calm temperament, you could look into what therapy dogs are doing in your area.

Therapy dogs go with their owners to visit patients at hospitals or nursing homes, generally remaining on leash but able to coax a pat from a stiffened hand, a smile from a blank face, a few words from sealed lips or a hug from someone in need of love.

Nursing homes cover a wide range of patient care. Some specialize in care of the elderly, some in the treatment of specific illnesses, some in physical therapy. Children's facilities also welcome visits from trained therapy dogs for boosting morale in their pediatric patients. Hospice care for the terminally ill and the at-home care of AIDS patients are other areas where this canine visiting is desperately needed. Therapy dog training comes first.

Your dog can make a differ-ence in lots of lives.

There is a lot more involved than just taking your nice friendly pooch to someone's bedside. Doing therapy dog work involves your own emotional stability as well as that of your dog. But once you have met all the requirements for this work, making the rounds once a week or once a month with your therapy dog is possibly the most rewarding of all community activities.

Disaster Aid

This community service is definitely not for everyone, partly because it is time-consuming. The initial training is rigorous, and there can be no let-up in the continuing workouts, because members are on call 24 hours a day to go wherever they are needed at a moment's notice. But if you think you would like to be able to assist in a disaster, look into search-and-rescue work. The network of search-and-rescue volunteers is worldwide, and all members of the American Rescue Dog Association (ARDA) who are qualified to do this work are volunteers who train and maintain their own dogs.

Physical Aid

Most people are familiar with Seeing Eye dogs, which serve as blind people's eyes, but not with all the other work that dogs are trained to do to assist the disabled. Dogs are also specially trained to pull wheelchairs, carry school books, pick up dropped objects, open and close doors. Some also are ears for the deaf. All these assistance-trained dogs, by the way, are allowed anywhere "No Pet" signs exist (as are therapy dogs when

properly identified). Getting started in any of this fascinating work requires a background in dog training and canine behavior, but there are also volunteer jobs ranging from answering the phone to cleaning out kennels to providing a foster home for a puppy. You have only to ask.

Making the rounds with your therapy dog can be very rewarding.

part four

Beyond
the
Basics

chapter 12

Recommended Reading

Books

ABOUT HEALTH CARE

Ackerman, Lowell. *Guide to Skin and Haircoat Problems in Dogs.* Loveland, Colo.: Alpine Publications, 1994.

Alderton, David. *The Dog Care Manual.* Hauppauge, N.Y.: Barron's Educational Series, Inc., 1986.

American Kennel Club. *American Kennel Club Dog Care and Training.* New York· Howell Book House, 1991.

Bamberger, Michelle, DVM. *Help! The Quick Guide to First Aid for Your Dog.* New York: Howell Book House, 1995.

Carlson, Delbert, DVM, and James Giffin, MD. *Dog Owner's Home Veterinary Handbook.* New York: Howell Book House, 1992.

DeBitetto, James, DVM, and Sarah Hodgson. *You & Your Puppy.* New York: Howell Book House, 1995.

Humphries, Jim, DVM. *Dr. Jim's Animal Clinic for Dogs.* New York: Howell Book House, 1994.

McGinnis, Terri. *The Well Dog Book.* New York: Random House, 1991.

Pitcairn, Richard and Susan. *Natural Health for Dogs.* Emmaus, Pa.: Rodale Press, 1982.

ABOUT DOG SHOWS

Hall, Lynn. *Dog Showing for Beginners.* New York: Howell Book House, 1994.

Nichols, Virginia Tuck. *How to Show Your Own Dog.* Neptune, N. J.: TFH, 1970.

Vanacore, Connie. *Dog Showing, An Owner's Guide.* New York: Howell Book House, 1990.

ABOUT TRAINING

Ammen, Amy. *Training in No Time.* New York: Howell Book House, 1995.

Baer, Ted. *Communicating With Your Dog.* Hauppauge, N.Y.: Barron's Educational Series, Inc., 1989.

Benjamin, Carol Lea. *Dog Problems.* New York: Howell Book House, 1989.

Benjamin, Carol Lea. *Dog Training for Kids.* New York: Howell Book House, 1988.

Benjamin, Carol Lea. *Mother Knows Best.* New York: Howell Book House, 1985.

Benjamin, Carol Lea. *Surviving Your Dog's Adolescence.* New York: Howell Book House, 1993.

Bohnenkamp, Gwen. *Manners for the Modern Dog.* San Francisco: Perfect Paws, 1990.

Dibra, Bashkim. *Dog Training by Bash.* New York: Dell, 1992.

Dunbar, Ian, PhD, MRCVS. *Dr. Dunbar's Good Little Dog Book,* James & Kenneth Publishers, 2140 Shattuck Ave. #2406, Berkeley, Calif. 94704. (510) 658–8588. Order from the publisher.

Dunbar, Ian, PhD, MRCVS. *How to Teach a New Dog Old Tricks,* James & Kenneth Publishers. Order from the publisher; address above.

Dunbar, Ian, PhD, MRCVS, and Gwen Bohnenkamp. Booklets on *Preventing Aggression; Housetraining; Chewing; Digging; Barking; Socialization; Fearfulness; and Fighting,* James & Kenneth Publishers. Order from the publisher; address above.

Evans, Job Michael. *People, Pooches and Problems.* New York: Howell Book House, 1991.

Kilcommons, Brian and Sarah Wilson. *Good Owners, Great Dogs.* New York: Warner Books, 1992.

McMains, Joel M. *Dog Logic—Companion Obedience.* New York: Howell Book House, 1992.

Rutherford, Clarice and David H. Neil, MRCVS. *How to Raise a Puppy You Can Live With.* Loveland, Colo.: Alpine Publications, 1982.

Volhard, Jack and Melissa Bartlett. *What All Good Dogs Should Know: The Sensible Way to Train.* New York: Howell Book House, 1991.

ABOUT BREEDING

Harris, Beth J. Finder. *Breeding a Litter, The Complete Book of Prenatal and Postnatal Care.* New York: Howell Book House, 1983.

Holst, Phyllis, DVM. *Canine Reproduction.* Loveland, Colo.: Alpine Publications, 1985.

Walkowicz, Chris and Bonnie Wilcox, DVM. *Successful Dog Breeding, The Complete Handbook of Canine Midwifery*. New York: Howell Book House, 1994.

ABOUT ACTIVITIES

American Rescue Dog Association. *Search and Rescue Dogs*. New York: Howell Book House, 1991.

Barwig, Susan and Stewart Hilliard. *Schutzhund*. New York: Howell Book House, 1991.

Beaman, Arthur S. *Lure Coursing*. New York: Howell Book House, 1994.

Daniels, Julie. *Enjoying Dog Agility—From Backyard to Competition*. New York: Doral Publishing, 1990.

Davis, Kathy Diamond. *Therapy Dogs*. New York: Howell Book House, 1992.

Gallup, Davis Anne. *Running With Man's Best Friend*. Loveland, Colo.: Alpine Publications, 1986.

Habgood, Dawn and Robert. *On the Road Again With Man's Best Friend*. New England, Mid-Atlantic, West Coast and Southeast editions. Selective guides to area bed and breakfasts, inns, hotels and resorts that welcome guests and their dogs. New York: Howell Book House, 1995.

Holland, Vergil S. *Herding Dogs*. New York: Howell Book House, 1994.

LaBelle, Charlene G. *Backpacking With Your Dog*. Loveland, Colo.: Alpine Publications, 1993.

Simmons-Moake, Jane. *Agility Training, The Fun Sport for All Dogs*. New York: Howell Book House, 1991.

Spencer, James B. *Hup! Training Flushing Spaniels the American Way*. New York: Howell Book House, 1992.

Spencer, James B. *Point! Training the All-Seasons Birddog*. New York: Howell Book House, 1995.

Tarrant, Bill. *Training the Hunting Retriever*. New York: Howell Book House, 1991.

Volhard, Jack and Wendy. *The Canine Good Citizen*. New York: Howell Book House, 1994.

General Titles

Haggerty, Captain Arthur J. *How to Get Your Pet Into Show Business*. New York: Howell Book House, 1994.

McLennan, Bardi. *Dogs and Kids, Parenting Tips*. New York: Howell Book House, 1993.

Moran, Patti J. *Pet Sitting for Profit, A Complete Manual for Professional Success*. New York: Howell Book House, 1992.

Scalisi, Danny and Libby Moses. *When Rover Just Won't Do, Over 2,000 Suggestions for Naming Your Dog*. New York: Howell Book House, 1993.

Sife, Wallace, PhD. *The Loss of a Pet*. New York: Howell Book House, 1993.

Wrede, Barbara J. *Civilizing Your Puppy*. Hauppauge, N.Y.: Barron's Educational Series, 1992.

Magazines

The AKC GAZETTE, The Official Journal for the Sport of Purebred Dogs. American Kennel Club, 51 Madison Ave., New York, NY.

Bloodlines Journal. United Kennel Club, 100 E. Kilgore Rd., Kalamazoo, MI.

Dog Fancy. Fancy Publications, 3 Burroughs, Irvine, CA 92718

Dog World. Maclean Hunter Publishing Corp., 29 N. Wacker Dr., Chicago, IL 60606.

Videos

"SIRIUS Puppy Training," by Ian Dunbar, PhD, MRCVS. James & Kenneth Publishers, 2140 Shattuck Ave. #2406, Berkeley, CA 94704. Order from the publisher.

"Training the Companion Dog," from Dr. Dunbar's British TV Series, James & Kenneth Publishers. (See address above).

The American Kennel Club produces videos on every breed of dog, as well as on hunting tests, field trials and other areas of interest to purebred dog owners. For more information, write to AKC/Video Fulfillment, 5580 Centerview Dr., Suite 200, Raleigh, NC 27606.

chapter 13

Resources

Breed Clubs

Every breed recognized by the American Kennel Club has a national (parent) club. National clubs are a great source of information on your breed. You can get the name of the secretary of the club by contacting:

The American Kennel Club
51 Madison Avenue
New York, NY 10010
(212) 696-8200

There are also numerous all-breed, individual breed, obedience, hunting and other special-interest dog clubs across the country. The American Kennel Club can provide you with a geographical list of clubs to find ones in your area. Contact them at the above address.

Registry Organizations

Registry organizations register purebred dogs. The American Kennel Club is the oldest and largest in this country, and currently recognizes over 130 breeds. The United Kennel Club registers some breeds the AKC doesn't (including the American Pit Bull Terrier and the Miniature Fox Terrier) as well as many of the same breeds. The others included here are for your reference; the AKC can provide you with a list of foreign registries.

American Kennel Club
51 Madison Avenue
New York, NY 10010

United Kennel Club (UKC)
100 E. Kilgore Road
Kalamazoo, MI 49001-5598

American Dog Breeders Assn.
P.O. Box 1771
Salt Lake City, UT 84110
(Registers American Pit Bull Terriers)

Canadian Kennel Club
89 Skyway Avenue
Etobicoke, Ontario
Canada M9W 6R4

National Stock Dog Registry
P.O. Box 402
Butler, IN 46721
(Registers working stock dogs)

Orthopedic Foundation for Animals (OFA)
2300 E. Nifong Blvd.
Columbia, MO 65201-3856
(Hip registry)

Activity Clubs

Write to these organizations for information on the activities they sponsor.

American Kennel Club
51 Madison Avenue
New York, NY 10010
(Conformation Shows, Obedience Trials, Field Trials and Hunting Tests, Agility, Canine Good

Citizen, Lure Coursing, Herding, Tracking,
Earthdog Tests, Coonhunting.)

United Kennel Club
100 E. Kilgore Road
Kalamazoo, MI 49001-5598
(Conformation Shows, Obedience Trials, Agility,
Hunting for Various Breeds, Terrier Trials and
more.)

North American Flyball Assn.
1342 Jeff St.
Ypsilanti, MI 48198

International Sled Dog Racing Assn.
P.O. Box 446
Norman, ID 83848-0446

North American Working Dog Assn., Inc.
Southeast Kreisgruppe
P.O. Box 833
Brunswick, GA 31521

Trainers

Association of Pet Dog Trainers
P.O. Box 3734
Salinas, CA 93912
(408) 663–9257

American Dog Trainers' Network
161 West 4th St.
New York, NY 10014
(212) 727–7257

**National Association of Dog Obedience
Instructors**
2286 East Steel Rd.
St. Johns, MI 48879

Associations

American Dog Owners Assn.
1654 Columbia Tpk.
Castleton, NY 12033
(Combats anti-dog legislation)

Delta Society
P.O. Box 1080
Renton, WA 98057-1080
(Promotes the human/animal bond through
pet-assisted therapy and other programs)

Dog Writers Assn. of America (DWAA)
Sally Cooper, Secy.
222 Woodchuck Ln.
Harwinton, CT 06791

National Assn. for Search and Rescue (NASAR)
P.O. Box 3709
Fairfax, VA 22038

Therapy Dogs International
6 Hilltop Road
Mendham, NJ 07945